# American Painted Porcelain

## COLLECTOR'S IDENTIFICATION & VALUE GUIDE

### Dorothy Kamm

## COLLECTOR BOOKS

*A Division of Schroeder Publishing Co., Inc.*

The current values in this book should be used only as a guide. They are not intended to set prices, which vary from one section of the country to another. Auction prices as well as dealer prices vary greatly and are affected by condition as well as demand. Neither the Author nor the Publisher assumes responsibility for any losses that might be incurred as a result of consulting this guide.

## Searching For A Publisher?

We are always looking for knowledgeable people considered to be experts within their fields. If you feel that there is a real need for a book on your collectible subject and have a large comprehensive collection, contact Collector Books.

## On the Cover:

Left to right: Lemonade pitcher, signed "C.N. Patterson, 1908," value: $175.00 – 225.00 (Plate 101); plate, signed "WANDS" (William D. Wands, Chicago, 1910 – 1916, value: $45.00 – 55.00 (Plate 76); creamer, signed "W. Wilson," ca. 1891 – 1914, value: $20.00 – 30.00 (Plate 152); jam jar, ca. 1880, value: $30.00–40.00 (Plate 144); vase, ca. 1906 – 1924, value: $250.00 – 300.00 (Plate 10); napkin ring, ca. 1880 – 1915, value $10.00 – 15.00 (Plate 88).

Cover design: Beth Summers
Book design: Joyce Cherry
Photography: Dorothy Kamm

Additional copies of this book may be ordered from:

COLLECTOR BOOKS
P.O. Box 3009
Paducah, Kentucky 42002-3009

@$19.95. Add $2.00 for postage and handling.

Printed in the U.S.A. by Image Graphics, Paducah, KY

# Contents

## Dedication

To my husband Dean, who always has been my best friend,
To my daughters Erica and Julia, who have provided me many reasons to leave behind a legacy that they can be proud of, and
To my parents, in-laws, students, and numerous friends who, when I presented my ideas and dreams, said three words that made all the difference to me —
**"Go for it!"**

## About the Author

Dorothy Kamm received a B.F.A. from Northern Illinois University, where she graduated with University Honors and with Honors in English, and an M.F.A. from the School of the Art Institute of Chicago. She became a porcelain artist certified and registered by the International Porcelain Artists and Teachers in 1990 after serving an apprenticeship, and her painted porcelains have been featured in *Victoria* and *Traditional Home* magazines. As an award-winning artist and author, Kamm is well-qualified to write and lecture because of her first-hand knowledge of china painting. She also publishes *Dorothy Kamm's Porcelain Collector's Companion,* a bi-monthly newsletter covering antique and contemporary hand painted porcelain.

Kamm lives in Port St. Lucie with her husband and two daughters. Since research is an on-going process, the exchange of ideas and information is welcome. Please accompany correspondence by a self-addressed, stamped envelope.

Dorothy Kamm
P.O. Box 7460
Port St. Lucie, FL 34985-7460

# Acknowledgments

There are many people who have helped me along the way — with encouragement, information, and assistance when needed. In particular, I thank my husband for his editorial comments; my parents Blanche and Irving Kampf, and my in-laws Miriam and Bernard Cohen, for their unceasing encouragement; my china painting students Mietta Ahlers, Michele Baggenstoss, Jean Jemmott, Judy Ladd, Adele Prince, Earleen Rowell, and Dorothy Szymanski for the forum they gave me when I read my manuscript during class; Dr. Shirley Dunbar for her expertise on the antiques marketplace, her observations, and for her editorial suggestions; Richard Rendall for providing me with a copy of Mary Louise McLaughlin's book, for his insights, his opinions, and his gifts of porcelain; Tim Ingram for sharing his knowledge, copies of his *Keramic Studio* magazines, and Thayer and Chandler catalogs; the students in my china painting class, as well as Roberta Deemer, for allowing me to discuss and sort through my ideas at length; Ruth Schroeder, for encouraging me to take the initial plunge and begin collecting antique hand painted porcelains; Beverly Rushin, for her expertise in library science and research methods; Jessica Kole, for her legal advice and accompanying me on antiquing expeditions; Michael Mudd, for his encouragement and gifts of porcelain; Dr. James D. Henderson, for performing and sharing research on Milwaukee china painters; and William Ayers, for his invaluable editorial comments.

I am indebted to the librarians of the St. Lucie County Public Library system, as well as to the following individuals and organizations for sharing their research: Laura Arksey, Curator of Special Collections, Cheney Cowles Museum/Eastern Washington State Historical Society in Spokane; Betty and the late Don Burbank of *The China Decorator* magazine; the Chicago Historical Society; Ellen Paul Denker; Raymond J. Fisher and the Eastern Washington Genealogical Society in Spokane; Erin Foley, Assistant Department Head, Special Collections, Minneapolis Public Library; Grace Gould, Research Volunteer at the Hennepin History Museum in Minneapolis; Ralph and Terry Kovel; Alan Reed; and Susan G. Rehkopf, Archivist, The Historical Society of University City, Missouri.

I also am indebted to Anne Wilder, Roberta Deemer, Dr. Shirley Dunbar, Mr. and Mrs. James G. Bowden III, and Bon Bon Antiques in Stuart, Florida, for allowing me to photograph their porcelains, and to the McFaddin-Ward House in Beaumont, Texas, for providing me with photographs.

Without the generosity of these people, this book would not have been successful. I thank all of you, and any others whom I may have inadvertently excluded.

# Foreword

Pottery has been collected since ancient times. The Romans treasured the best of the Greek vases. The rare cobalt blue Persian wares inspired the ceramists of later centuries. And everyone has heard the story of Marco Polo's trip to the Orient in the thirteenth century and his return with treasures from China that included porcelain tea cups. It led to the search for the secret of porcelain by craftsmen in Germany, France, and England.

Collecting is a passion, a romance, indeed some call it a disease. We were first infected during our courting days in college. By the time we married, porcelains had become an important part of our lives. In those days, antiques shows were held once a year in our city and house sales were rare. We haunted the few shops, ordered some rarities from England, and rushed each week to the few house sales to buy bargain pieces of 18th century English porcelain, old Chinese vases, and Meissen figurines. Our first book was *Kovels' Dictionary of Marks, Pottery and Porcelain,* written to help us identify the porcelains we were collecting.

Like all collectors those days, we ignored American art pottery, hand-painted plates, Fiesta ware, and old stoneware crocks and mixing bowls. By the 1970s, adventurous collectors had discovered art pottery and stoneware. We started searching for hand-painted Haviland-type art pottery, and porcelains decorated by the early women in the art pottery movement, like Mary Louise McLaughlin, Maria Longworth Nichols, and Mary Chase Perry. By the 1980s, Fiesta and other dinnerwares gained in favor. But it was not until the 1990s that hand-painted plates, first fashionable 100 years ago, by then-unidentified artists began to interest many collectors.

In our library there are over 16,000 books about antiques and collectibles. The ceramics section holds 1,147 books; 123 on art pottery, 89 on German porcelains, 63 on marks, but not one on hand-painted porcelains. Our major sources of information have been copies of old china-painting magazines and six years of the newsletter "Dorothy Kamm's Porcelain Collector's Companion."

Look through this book, *American Painted Porcelain: Collector's Identification & Value Guide,* carefully and study the pictures as well as the text. The collector of painted porcelains must rely on personal taste and an ability to recognize quality work. Train your eye. You can still find wonderful examples of the artistry of the many women and men who painted china in America. The information needed to identify these pieces can be found in this important book by Dorothy Kamm. The history of painted porcelain is here, including a chronology of events, explanations of painting styles, colors preferred, techniques used, important artists and schools of painting, and types of porcelains selected. Diagrams explain how to recognize the work of a talented artist—diagrams that could have been drawn only by an author who has spent years as a china decorating artist. The lengthy bibliography includes old and new books and publications. An alphabetical list of artists and studios is included for quick reference. Color pictures show over 150 quality pieces. Absorb all this information, then start your search for the best of the hand-painted porcelain treasures and bargains.

Ralph and Terry Kovel

# Preface

Collectors and antique dealers have only recently "discovered" American hand painted porcelain, and they are just becoming aware of its history, beauty, and potential value. Others who have inherited family heirlooms want to know more about what they have. People with historic homes look for decorative accessories, such as American painted porcelains, to lend an air of authenticity to their interiors. Others simply appreciate the uniqueness of these one-of-a-kind artworks. Curators and historians have taken an active interest in this part of American decorative art history, and china painting has been featured with increasing frequency in special exhibitions.

Little did I know how a partial set of dinnerware given to me by my grandfather during my teenage years would influence my future. Every day that my family used the set, I thought about learning to paint on porcelain to create the missing pieces. Despite these constant reminders, it took me four years to find a teacher, and another ten years to begin lessons. It wasn't until my first child was nine months old that I learned to paint on porcelain, and this was eight years after I had last picked up a paint brush!

What started as a pastime soon turned into a passion. Not long after I began painting, my attention turned towards exploring the history of this exciting art. I discovered that dozens of books already had been published on most major European and Asian porcelain factories and studios, but very little on the American movement. Although some information was available concerning major manufacturers and decorators, I found no cohesive source that documented the history of the American china painting movement, and the many people who influenced it. This book is the culmination of nearly a decade of research. Its intent is to appeal to a broad audience, from the novice who inherits family porcelain treasures, to the advanced collector and dealer. It is my hope that this book will serve as a reference, an art gallery, and a tribute to those anonymous artists who left behind such a beautiful and wide-ranging legacy.

From its beginnings, quality pieces commensurate with their European counterparts were produced. While European porcelains often cost hundreds and thousands of dollars, American pieces of equal quality can be purchased for a fraction of that. Collecting American painted porcelain is well within the budget of most people. Initially decorated for a middle class market, it is still affordably priced. Most pieces can be purchased for less than one hundred dollars. This means paying as little as ten dollars for a six-inch plate, and less than fifty dollars for many other items. These two factors – availability and price – are key to making American painted porcelain a desired collectible.

# Introduction

The history of a nation is reflected most beautifully in its artistic accomplishments. Painting on porcelain, though it has had a very short history in America, was one such artistic contribution that played an important cultural role in the late nineteenth and early twentieth centuries. Whereas only the rich and royalty could afford porcelain in the eighteenth century, technological advancements developed a century later during the Industrial Revolution made it possible for factories to increase porcelain output without sacrificing quality, while at the same time making undecorated porcelain more affordable.

Porcelain painting as an art form practiced separately from its manufacture had a modest start in the early 1870s. The turning point for its rise in popularity was the United States Centennial Exposition held in Philadelphia in 1876. On display in the Woman's Pavilion were numerous porcelains that had been painted by art students in Cincinnati. Millions of people who attended the Exposition were exposed to American china painting for the first time, and many were excited by this new art. Eventually, thousands learned to china paint, while others supported china painters through their purchases.

China painting became a career for some and a chance for creative expression for many — particularly women — in the late nineteenth and early twentieth centuries. Although more than 20,000 women painted porcelain one hundred years ago, a majority of them have been labeled as amateurs, implying artistic incompetence.

The word "amateur" is derived from the Latin root "amare," which means to love. An amateur, then, is a person who pursues an activity out of love rather than for profit. No one can doubt the amateur talent of the painter Samuel F. B. Morse, who also invented the telegraph and Morse code, or the printer Benjamin Franklin who invented the Franklin stove and helped write the Constitution.

Were the women who practiced the art of china painting just dabblers? Although many of them did not have the extensive art training of their male counterparts who learned their craft in Europe, they had the passion, drive, involvement, and persistence that fine artists share. We can judge their talent by the myriad plates, pitchers, and other porcelain paraphernalia that they left behind.

Why has American painted porcelain been so undervalued until recently? The functional aspect of the wares tended to override aesthetics. This in turn created an identity crisis, one with which this country has long contended. Additionally, the decorative arts have not enjoyed the same status as artworks executed in more traditional mediums. Though officially declared a fine art in 1976 by the office of President Jimmy Carter, painted porcelain has not gained the same respect that it has long maintained in Europe and in the Orient.

A nation that values only that which it does not create, rejecting productions of its own, is bound to fail in its endeavors, and that is exactly what happened to American painted porcelain. Often equal in quality to china decorated by European artists, it seems that the only qualification American pieces lacked was that the painted product did not travel thousands of miles to reach our country.

The American china painting movement experienced numerous declines and resurgences throughout its history. Weaknesses became evident as early as 1895 when its catalyst, Mary Louise McLaughlin, became the first of several leaders to abandon the art (see Chronology, page 11). A major blow was dealt when wares decorated by amateur American china painters were barred from competition at the World's Fair held in Paris in 1901, demonstrating the obvious lack of respect given to these women and their work. World War I, followed by the Great Depression, basically strangled and suffocated the art form.

Investing in porcelain tableware and decorative objects, important status and artistic symbols in the late nineteenth and early twentieth centuries, is again finding renewed interest as we near the dawn of a new century. Since whiteware used by contemporary porcelain artists may be copied from antique pieces and techniques and materials have remained virtually unchanged for hundreds of years, classifying the origin and date of a piece can be a difficult proposition. This book is designed to give both advanced and beginning collectors an organized approach in acquiring and evaluating American painted porcelain.

Most of the American painted porcelain available in today's antique marketplace dates from the peak years of the movement — from 1885 to as late as the early 1930s. However, identifying American painted porcelain is often confounded by foreign factory backstamps. Those who pursued china painting found it necessary to employ imported blanks (undecorated, glazed white porcelain) from Europe because porcelain production never developed into a major industry in this country. The subject and style of the painting are often the only indicators of origin. There are times, though, when similarities between European and American decorating styles hinder the identification process. Additionally, the artists themselves, as well as their families, rarely kept records, for they did not realize the value their artworks would possess to future generations. Without records, exact dating is impossible. One can only draw reasonable conclusions based on the date of the backstamp, the painting subject and its style of portrayal, and the color palette. Chapter 3 has been written to assist readers with the classification process.

Developing expertise takes time. Today's collectors must approach the marketplace with savvy to avoid costly mistakes. This includes familiarity with the movement's history, and knowledge about the manufacture and decoration of porcelain, which can be gleaned from the first two chapters of this book.

Collectors must establish their own system of determining artistic quality because they cannot rely on "name brands," i.e., artists who are well known and well documented. Chapter 4 provides relevant information in an easy-to-follow format on employing research and cataloging methods using various tools of the trade to document artists wherever possible. Lastly, time spent reading pertinent publications, visiting historical homes and museums, and joining historical societies listed in Chapter 6 and at the end of the book will give collectors, dealers, curators, and historians greater understanding of this unique artistic medium and its role in American society.

*The decoration of china is a peculiarly interesting art, because by this means articles that are both beautiful and useful can be produced, and also in that the mineral decoration, once fixed by fire, is fadeless and invulnerable to the ravages of time as long as the object upon which it is applied endures.*

> Mary Louise McLaughlin
> *opening paragraph in*
> The China Painters' Hand Book
> (1917)

*The great aim of the decorator should be the solution of this problem:  given, a thing of beauty; make it still more beautiful.*

> L. Vance-Phillips
> Book of the China Painter
> (1896)

# Chronology

1871 — German immigrant Karl Lagenbeck, who resides in Cincinnati, Ohio, receives set of china paints from German uncle, and is assisted in experimentation by his neighbor Maria Longworth Nichols; although Lagenbeck asserted no influence on the china painting movement, Nichols's participation was consequential

1874 — Student art exhibition held at the McMicken School of Design in Cincinnati; on display are painted porcelains executed by Maria Longworth Nichols; Mary Louise McLaughlin admires this work and asks art instructor Benn Pitman to purchase supplies during his forthcoming trip to New York; Pitman organizes an extracurricular china painting class in early summer for interested students; taught by Dresden-trained porcelain artist Marie Eggers

1875 — Cincinnati Centennial Tea Party held in May; over 200 hand painted porcelain tea cups and saucers painted by students in Eggers's class auctioned at this student fund-raiser, encouraging them to continue their pursuit of the art of china painting, and to prepare an exhibit for the Centennial Exposition

1876 — The United States Centennial Exposition held in Philadelphia, Pennsylvania, from May 10 to November 10; examples of painted china produced by Eggers's students on display in the Woman's Pavilion; over one million visitors attended the Exposition, launching the American china painting movement

1877 — Mary Louise McLaughlin publishes *China Painting: A Practical Manual for the Use of Amateurs in the Decoration of Hard Porcelain*; over the years several editions published, selling 23,000 copies in all; *Hints on Household Taste* by Charles Locke Eastlake published in the United States, spreading the Aesthetic Movement from England to the United States, and advocating that a tastefully decorated home be filled with artistically-designed utilitarian and decorative items

1878 — Osgood Art School, the first school for china painters, is established in New York City by Adelaide Harriett Osgood

1879 — Woman's Pottery Club formed in Cincinnati with 15 members, McLaughlin as first president; this club becomes the model on which other ceramic clubs across the United States are organized; *The Art Amateur*, a magazine devoted to the cultivation of household arts, begins publication

1880 — First exhibition and sale of Woman's Pottery Club held in May, featuring about 200 pieces

1883 — *Ladies' Home Journal* begins publication; Susan Stuart Goodrich Frackelton establishes Frackelton China Decorating Works in Milwaukee, firing 1,500 to 2,000 pieces a week with the help of a decorating staff

1885 — World's Industrial and Cotton Centennial Exposition, Atlanta, Georgia; Frackelton is awarded a gold and a silver medal for her china paintings; Frackelton publishes her book *Tried by Fire*; Adelaide Alsop (Robineau) begins teaching china painting in Faribault, Minnesota; *Good Housekeeping* begins publication

1886 — Frackelton patents a portable, gas-fired kiln

1887 — *The China Decorator*, a magazine devoted to china painting, begins publication

1888 — Osgood publishes *How to Apply Royal Worcester Matt Bronze, LaCroix and Dresden Colors to China*

1889 — McLaughlin is awarded a silver medal at the Paris *Exposition Universelle* for her overglaze decoration with metallic effects; Benjamin Harrison is elected president of the United States; his wife Caroline starts a china painting class in the White House attended by herself, family members, and personal friends; donates her own porcelain artworks to numerous charitable causes

1890 — Mary Chase Perry opens a studio on West Adams Street in Detroit, Michigan; forms partnership with neighbor Horace J. Caulkins to develop and market a portable and economical kiln for china painters; Cincinnati's Woman's Pottery Club disbands

1891 — Cincinnati's Woman's Pottery Club reorganizes to begin production on wares to be exhibited in the Woman's Building at the upcoming World's Columbian Exposition

1892 — National League of Mineral Painters founded by Frackelton

1893 — World's Columbian Exposition, Chicago, Illinois, is held from May 1 to October 30; examples of china paintings displayed in the Woman's Pavilion

1894 — Frackelton, who developed and marketed Frackelton Dry Water Colors, earns numerous medals and a special award at the *Exposition Universelle d'Anvers* held in Antwerp, Belgium, for her gold and bronze colors

1895 — McLaughlin abandons china painting in favor of art pottery, which offers greater challenges

1896 — *House Beautiful* begins publication in December; L. Vance Phillips, a contributing writer for china painting column in *The Art Amateur* magazine, publishes *Book of the China Painter*

1899 — Robineau, with her new husband Samuel, begins publishing *Keramic Studio* in May, Syracuse, New York; around 1900 the School of the Art Institute of Chicago and the Pennsylvania Museum School of Industrial Art in Philadelphia begin offering china painting classes

1901 — World's Fair held in Paris; amateur American painted china barred from competition; *House & Garden* begins publication; *The China Decorator* ceases publication

1902 — Frackelton abandons china painting for unclear reasons; *The Art Amateur* no longer features articles on china painting, although the magazine still publishes patterns and carries advertising geared to the china painting market

1903 — Perry and Robineau abandon china painting in favor of art pottery, where they have greater control of the creative process, and receive greater recognition for their efforts and accomplishment; *The Art Amateur* ceases publication

1908 — American Woman's League founded by publisher Edward G. Lewis; free correspondence courses, including china painting, are offered to members in exchange for sales of magazine subscriptions

1910 — Publisher Edward G. Lewis develops University City near St. Louis, Missouri, establishing The People's University; Mrs. Kathryn E. Cherry is one china painting instructor in the School of Ceramic Art of the Art Academy

1911 — The People's University closes and the American Woman's League becomes defunct

1912 — Dorothea Warren O'Hara, who was a master of enamel decoration which became known as American Satsuma, publishes *The Art of Enameling on Porcelain*

1913 — Elsie de Wolfe writes *The House in Good Taste*; advocates getting rid of Victorian clutter — including decorative porcelains — and streamlining one's household

1914 — Outbreak of World War I, restricting export of china and supplies

1915 — O'Hara wins several gold medals at the Panama-Pacific Exposition in San Francisco, California; two of her vases are bought by the Japanese government; an exhibit of twelve rooms designed and accessorized to a single motif show the first signs of the melding of craftsmanship with industry, and the birth of the "modern," simplified style

1918 — World War I ends

1920 — O'Hara abandons china painting for pottery

1924 — *Keramic Studio* renamed *Design Keramic Studio* to appeal to a broader readership

1929 — A worldwide depression begins; *Design Keramic Studio* ceases publication

1933 — A Century of Progress Exposition opens in Chicago; hand painted porcelain is not part of any exhibits

1939 — World War II begins

1945 — World War II ends

1956 — Nettie Pillet begins publishing *The China Decorator*, which plays an instrumental role in revitalizing china painting

1958 — National China Painting Teachers Organization formed in Dallas with 13 members; this group later became the International Porcelain Artists and Teachers, Inc.

1967 — The World Organization of China Painters is founded by Pauline A. Salyer in Oklahoma City, Oklahoma

# Key Artists

Kathryn E. Cherry 1871 – 1931

Susan Stuart Goodrich Frackelton 1848 – 1932

Mary Louise McLaughlin 1847 – 1939

Maria Longworth Nichols 1849 – 1932

Dorothea Warren O'Hara 1875 – 1963

Adelaide Harriett Osgood 1842 – 1910

Mary Chase Perry (Stratton) 1868 – 1961

Adelaide Alsop Robineau 1865 – 1929

# Chapter One

## The History of American Painted Porcelain

### American Culture and Artistic Influences

In the early part of the nineteenth century, the decoration of porcelain was tied with its manufacture, and American factories emulated European porcelains. This was a result of our young nation's lacking a definitive and established artistic style, and a reflection of the immigrants employed in these factories. Having learned their crafts in their respective native lands, these artisans designed and painted in styles familiar to them. By the latter half of the nineteenth century, skilled porcelain painters who had emigrated to the United States, such as the noted George Leykauf of Detroit and Edward Lycett of New York City, opened their own studios and competed with American manufacturers by using imported whiteware. Although they gained reputations as expert artists and teachers, they were not the ones who proved most influential in the spread of the art form.

Cincinnati was the birthplace of the American china painting movement. There Karl Lagenbeck, a German immigrant and ceramic chemist, received as a gift a set of overglaze china paints from an uncle in Germany. His neighbor, Maria Longworth Nichols, assisted him in experimenting with these paints. As an art student at the McMicken School of Design, Nichols's successfully decorated porcelains were displayed at a student exhibition. Her classmate, Mary Louise McLaughlin, admired her work and asked their art instructor, Benn Pitman, to purchase the necessary supplies on his next trip to New York. Pitman obliged, organizing an extracurricular class for students who had expressed an interest in learning how to paint china.

Since china painting was a new medium in this country, Pitman procured Marie Eggers, a Dresden-trained porcelain artist, to teach a class in 1874. These students successfully painted a significant amount of porcelain, some of which was exhibited at the Woman's Pavilion at the Philadelphia Centennial Exposition. This in itself is amazing considering the tremendous skill required to become proficient at painting porcelain, as well as the length of time and multiple firing necessary to complete pieces. Millions who attended the Exposition were exposed to this new art form, and many embraced it.

### The Spread of China Painting

Several factors and key persons were influential in the acceptance of china painting as an occupation and art form in this country. China painting was a new and challenging medium, one whose novelty alone caused excitement. As public awareness of this field expanded, so did the market. Technological developments in the nineteenth century resulted in more efficient manufacturing techniques, reducing product costs, including those of porcelain. Whereas in the eighteenth century porcelain belonged only to the wealthy who could afford it, by the late nineteenth century fancy tableware, dresser sets, and various decorative accessories were routinely owned by middle class families as well. People who could afford to purchase hand painted porcelains imported from Europe now chose their patterns and their pieces from dozens of independent American china painters who operated studios across the country, or they could decorate porcelains themselves.

Ideals of the Aesthetic Movement, which started in England in the mid-nineteenth century, were broadcast by the Centennial Exposition and by progressives such as Pitman. Pitman was a disciple of art critic and philosopher John Ruskin and designer William Morris. They advocated, among other principles, that individually crafted items were artistically superior to machine-made objects. Furthermore, they believed in an aesthetic philosophy where everyday objects should be appreciated as works of art and advocated making one's home an oasis. Americans, already feeling the social pressures of mechanization, looked with longing at a romanticized past, one where handcrafted objects represented simpler times.

Many women turned to creative occupations which allowed them to beautify their homes with their own artistic creations, and painting on porcelain was one such outlet. It was socially acceptable to display one's wealth and good taste in one's own home. Then, too, one-of-a-kind craftworks personalized rooms generally furnished with mass-produced furniture and furnishings. Painted china became vehicles incorporating decorative arts into daily life as well as status symbols.

The American china painting movement flourished from the class taught by Eggers. This class launched the artistic careers of several students and influenced many others. Mary Louise McLaughlin, one of Eggers's students, was the catalyst of the American painted porcelain movement. She published her first book on china painting in 1877 to guide those working without the benefit of a teacher. When McLaughlin formed the Woman's Pottery Club in 1879, little did she dream that her passion for porcelain would influence an entire nation. This local club, whose purpose was to establish artistic standards and to promote the art, became the model for ceramic clubs established elsewhere.

McLaughlin and her club were also instrumental in attracting women from across the nation to study in Cincinnati. Returning to their hometowns they opened their own studios, and thus began the spread of china painting. By 1881 Chicago, Boston, Philadelphia, and New York City had become major china painting centers.

Whiteware and painting supplies were easily attainable from American shops and studios that imported these from Europe, but one of the difficulties china painters encountered was locating kilns to fire their pieces. Most painters had to ship their work to a limited number of large studios with firing facilities, a time-consuming process that sometimes resulted in damaged pieces. Mary Chase Perry, a Detroit-based porcelain artist, was instrumental in the development and distribution of a portable and economical kerosene-fueled kiln specifically geared to china painters.

Susan Stuart Goodrich Frackelton of Milwaukee also developed and patented a portable gas kiln for porcelain, in addition to writing and publishing the book *Tried by Fire* in 1885, and forming the National League of Mineral Painters in 1892. The League organized professional porcelain artists and strove to improve artistic standards through work, study, and annual exhibitions.

As publisher of *Keramic Studio* magazine, Adelaide Alsop Robineau was the person most responsible for propelling the china painting movement into the twentieth century. Founded in May 1899, the magazine was immediately successful. It became the official publication of the National League of Mineral Painters. An accomplished china painter and artist herself, Robineau used her influence to promote other women artists and the art form.

## The Decline and Resurgence of Porcelain Painting

Charting the rise of the porcelain painting movement from city directories shows the art peaked just prior to World War I when European imports, including the whiteware and supplies that American china painters depended upon, were restricted. (At the time, American-produced porcelain was unavailable to china painters, and Japanese whiteware was inferior.) But signs of distress had occurred even earlier. The Woman's Pottery Club, once the most influential club of its kind, disbanded in 1890 due to lack of funding. Though over 20,000 people practiced china painting, by 1900 the National League of Mineral Painters had attracted only 500 members; it never realized its goal of establishing a national china painting school.

Streams of immigrants from England, France, Austria, and Germany, trained as porcelain artists under the tutelage of traditional apprentice systems established for over a century in their respective homelands, began arriving in greater numbers in the 1880s and 1890s. Within a relatively short time they opened studios where they offered lessons, supplies, and finished pieces to an eager American market. These male artists were immediately recognized as professionals, while the American women artists were looked upon as mere amateurs both in ability and pursuit. Further hindering the women were their production differences. Europeans trained in factories learned that speed was as important as technique. To the American artists who valued experimentation, creativity and individual expression overrode time concerns. Limited production, of course, resulted in limited income.

Around the turn of the twentieth century, romanticism, with its sympathetic interest in nature, was being usurped by a modern design attitude, one that preferred abstract and conventional motifs, and simpler, uncluttered settings. Many painters clung to a more traditional style, and their paintings began to look dated. Some of the most talented were frustrated by what they perceived as the limitations of the medium and the low status given to porcelain painters and abandoned china painting altogether. Lastly, and perhaps most importantly, numerous practitioners found that because of the time consuming process involved in creating and completing finished paintings, they could not earn a sufficient living.

The Depression and World War II further eroded the movement. Those who pursued china painting as a hobby — and they were in the majority — stopped when discretionary income and imports decreased. Modern aesthetic trends, coupled with pressures for speed and mass-production, were destructive to this more traditional art form, as well as to producing quality artwork. Porcelain painting was virtually extinct and the handful of practitioners disorganized until 1958 when a group of 13 women in Dallas formed a club that is still active. This International Porcelain Artists and Teachers, together with the World Organization of China Painters based in Oklahoma City, boasts a combined membership of over 9,000 china painters in the United States. American painted porcelain once again is taking an esteemed place in our history and in our homes.

# Chapter Two

## Porcelain Production and Decoration

### Manufacture of Porcelain

The manufacture of porcelain is a complex and expensive undertaking. True porcelain is a semi-vitrified compound of kaolin, a fine, white clay that forms when rocks containing feldspar (aluminum silicate) decompose through weathering, and petuntse, which is a china stone made from decomposed granite. When fired, kaolin remains plastic but infusible — i.e., it doesn't melt — while petuntse becomes glasslike and transparent, enveloping the infusible part. As a result, the clay becomes smooth, compact, and translucent. Without glaze, however, the surface remains rough, dull in appearance, and quite porous. Glaze is a colorless, thin coating of lead or alkaline, often mixed with feldspar. When fired, it fuses with the porcelain and encloses the clay with a waterproof layer of glass.

A variety of problems and setbacks can occur during firing. These include sagging, shrinking, or collapsing of the original forms. Despite these drawbacks, the finished product is unique in a number of ways. Unlike any other clay product, porcelain is translucent. Its texture is smoother and finer, its color a bright white. When tapped, porcelain produces a resonant, bell-like ring. Last of all its high tensile strength allows delicate, molded forms which can be eggshell-thin.

### Discovery of Porcelain

Historians contend that porcelain was introduced into Europe upon Marco Polo's return from China in 1275. This new type of pottery called *porcellana* (because of its resemblance to the cowrie shell), immediately became highly desirable as an important item to Europe, while European pottery remained crude in comparison. When the seaway to the East Indies was discovered after the circumnavigation of the Cape of Good Hope in 1497, porcelain began to appear in Europe with increasing frequency. The china trade flourished when the Dutch established their East Indian Company in 1602. With this influx, porcelain gained prominence as a coveted commodity. Although the Chinese had been producing porcelain for centuries, they retained their monopoly by limiting exports and foreign access to their country. This, coupled with excessive royal demand, inflated the price of porcelain to a status competitive with gold. Porcelain thus became regarded as "white gold."

Although countless attempts were made to establish porcelain production in Europe, several factors stifled success for centuries. The Chinese, realizing the value of their monopoly, were protective of the secret of porcelain production. When asked about its manufacture, they claimed that porcelain was made from eggshells, seashells, and other ingredients that were mixed together and buried for 80 to 100 years. This bit of misinformation kept Europeans off track for two centuries!

Secondly, only a few places in the world have kaolin deposits, including Saxony, Germany; China; and Cornwall, England, a factor which directly influenced the development and production of porcelain. Lastly, a high kiln temperature ranging from 2,280 to 2,370 degrees Fahrenheit is required to fuse the clay. About one thousand years before the Europeans, the Chinese developed the most elaborate and sophisticated kilns capable of producing these high temperatures.

In Saxony, Germany, Johann Friedrich Böttger, along with the royal physicist Ehrenfried Walther Tschirnhausen, was credited with uncovering the Chinese "secret" of porcelain production. Discovered in 1708, it took an additional five years to perfect and improve the formula employed for over a millennium by the Chinese.

In America, porcelain production never developed into a major decorative art industry. Though numerous firms manufactured many beautiful porcelain pieces, limited export markets and higher manufacturing costs restricted their success. Due to this lack of undecorated American-made whiteware, china painters worked on blanks imported from Germany, France, and Austria. Other supplies also were imported.

### Methods of Decoration

As a canvas, porcelain is coveted as much for its white color as for its fineness. Although porcelain's origins are traced back to the T'ang dynasty (618 – 906 A.D.), it wasn't until the reign of Emperor Chenghua (1465 – 1487) that overglaze decoration was invented.

**Overglaze paints** — also called mineral colors — were derived from metallic salts. Different combinations of these metallic salts, including iron, zinc, and cobalt, created a plethora of colors that, when combined with a flux, rendered the colors fusible when heated. Flux was a glaze made from borax, flint, and lead. When heated, it formed what was essentially colored glass. Flux gave overglaze paints their characteristic soft sheen when fired, toning down the high shine of glazed porcelain.

Mineral colors either came in vials of powder that required grinding and mixing with a special oil, or premixed in tubes that needed no preparation. Special brushes made from squirrel hair were used to apply paint. These colors required kiln firing for maturation and permanency. Like the porcelain they covered, these paints were translucent. To build up depth of color and detail required numerous applications, as shown in Figure 1. All overglaze paints were vitrifiable. During each firing, where the kiln temperature ranged from about 1,375 to 1,550 degrees Fahrenheit, the glaze softened, then fused with the paint as the kiln cooled.

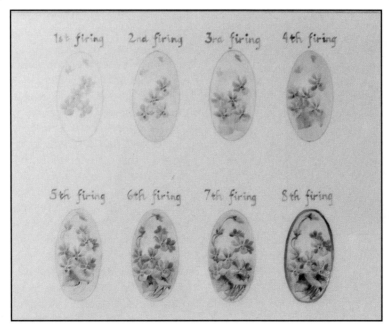

Figure 1
*Mineral colors required kiln firing for maturation and permanency. Like the porcelain they covered, these paints were translucent. Building up depth of color and detail required numerous applications.*

Figure 2
*Matt paints left a dull, velvet-like opaque surface that completely concealed the texture and glaze of porcelain. Using a s'graffito technique, the artist of this piece "carved" her cipher and the year she decorated the piece into the paint on the base of this powder box.*

Artists sometimes used matt paints. **Matt paints**, which contained no flux, left a dull, velvet-like, opaque surface devoid of any luster (Figure 2). They completely concealed the texture and glaze of porcelain. Since matt paints were prone to grease stains, they were usually limited to background tinting. A dry-grounding technique was employed when applied. First the porcelain's surface was covered with a grounding oil, such as Oil of Copaiba, and padded with silk wrapped around a piece of wool until it was slightly "tacky." After the grounding oil set, powdered color was dusted on with a large blending brush, and excess color gently brushed off. Matt colors also were used in conjunction with gold and other metals for contrasting effects.

Sometimes paintings were enhanced with thick, opaque **enamels and raised paste** for three-dimensional effects, as seen in Figure 3. Enamels, which were white or pre-tinted, were used to embellish a painting, such as adding a water-like effect on underwater scenes or enhancing petal edges. In tinted form they also were used to simulate jewels. Raised paste, which fired yellow in color, was employed only as a basis for gold application. Both enamel and raised paste were applied in dots, scrolls, or lines with a thin liner brush or stylus.

**Gilding** — the application of gold — was used to finish decorated pieces. There were several types of gold that china painters could employ (Figure 4). Roman gold was thicker and had a higher gold content. After firing, it displayed a dull ocher color. Burnishing (polishing) either with a glass brush, an agate, or scouring with fine white sand was required to bring out a soft sheen. Bright gold came in liquid form and fired with a high shine. It was more like a luster than true gold. Bright gold was not used as much in old porcelains because its finish was considered garish. By mixing other metals with gold, several color variations occurred. These included green gold, red gold, and white gold.

**Silver and platinum** were also used, though not as often because color trends and the color of available lighting, including gaslight, candles, and kerosene lamps, favored warmer tones. Although both silver and platinum were shiny, platinum did not tarnish. All metals were brushed on.

As an alternative to covering borders with solid gild-

Figure 3

*Enamels, which were available in white and various colors, were used to embellish paintings. On the lid of this powder box turquoise-colored enamel dots were used to simulate jewels. Raised paste, which was employed only as a basis for gold, was used to create a beaded border for the gilded band.*

Figure 4

*The inside of this powder box is lined with bright gold. In contrast, Roman gold, which has a softer appearance, was used as a border accent on the outside rims of the bottom and the lid.*

ing, areas first could be **etched.** Etched designs were drawn in tar (also called asphaltum). When dipped in hydrofluoric acid, the design covered with tar was protected from the acid, while the glaze in the uncovered portions was eaten away. After gold was applied and fired, etched areas presented contrasting patterns of shiny and dull surfaces, as seen in Figure 5.

**Lusters** were made from the same minerals as over-

The last category of decoration includes the combination of photography and hand painting. The nationally renowned, Atlanta-based china painters William Lycett and his son Edward collaborated with a local photographer to perfect the process of firing photographic images directly onto china. Though the exact date of their accomplishment is not known, the technique became popular during the 1890s.

> *Porcelain artists also could purchase pre-etched porcelains from supply companies. For example, Thayer & Chandler, a Chicago-based china supplier, advertised acid etched china in a rose design, similar to the one pictured in Figure 5, in its September 1, 1919 catalog.*

**Figure 5**
*Etched designs were created by first protecting the designs with tar, then dipping the porcelain into hydrofluoric acid. The uncovered portions were eaten away by the acid, producing contrasting patterns of shiny and dull surfaces.*

**Figure 6**
*Lusters added iridescent accents that shimmered like sunlight flashing across dragonfly wings. Mother-of-pearl was the most prevalent luster chosen to cover porcelain surfaces, though a variety of colors ranging from pastels to deep jewel tones was available.*

glaze colors, but were mixed with balsam of sulfur and thinned oil of turpentine, forming a liquid that held the metal in suspension. Lusters were available in a variety of colors, though mother-of-pearl was most commonly used. Like paints and metals, lusters were applied with a brush. When fired, these resulted in a lustrous and iridescent effect best limited to backgrounds and border bands (Figure 6).

Gold, silver, and lusters never fused with the glaze as mineral colors did, and thus, were not permanent. Typically, porcelains decorated with them may show signs of wear because these materials literally rubbed off with time.

## Design and Application

Initially, porcelain artists created their own studies for china paintings directly from natural models. They either transferred their drawings by directly sketching on the porcelain with a pencil or a paint brush, or by tracing a pattern onto porcelain with carbon paper from a sketch first drawn on tracing paper (Figure 7). Paints were applied with a variety of specialized brushes (Figure 8). By the early twentieth century several aids were marketed, enabling individuals less artistically inclined to decorate porcelain. Teachers began furnishing and renting their own watercolor studies. Eventually some studies were professionally printed and advertised in magazines such as *Keramic Studio* and *Ladies' Home Journal* to a national market. Many painters also directly copied designs printed in these magazines. Companies such as The Herrick Designs Company sold patterns that could be traced onto china without the use of carbon paper. Another company, F. G. Coover, promoted the use of their decal outlines to increase the art form's appeal, attract new students, and make china painting more profitable. Although decals offered standardization and perfection, in addition to quicker execution, aesthetically they reduced china painting to a craft that required little skill other than the ability to fill in blank spaces with flat areas of color. While increasing appeal, these diluted the

Photo courtesy of The McFaddin-Ward House, Beaumont, Texas

Figure 7

*Using carbon paper, drawings were transferred onto porcelain after a sketch was first drawn onto tracing paper. Pictured here are design tracings and painted porcelains from a set decorated by Mamie Louise McFaddin as a teenager in Beaumont, Texas. The blanks represent a mixture of French, German, and Austrian manufacturers.*

china painting movement and removed originality from the art form (Figure 9A and 9B). Vitrifiable decals, also called mineral transfers, were printed with mineral colors from lithographic stones onto paper backing. China was brushed with a special medium, usually oil of turpentine, and allowed to become tacky before decals were applied. The decal was then trimmed and placed face down on the china. Next, it was pressed with a damp cloth and burnished firmly with a small rubber roller. When the paper backing had been thoroughly dampened, it was carefully lifted off, leaving the mineral film design intact. Decals could be touched up or embellished by hand after firing.

This practice was usually limited to commercial studios wishing to save time and labor, illustrated by the plate in Figure 10. These pieces are often incorrectly identified as hand _painted_, rather than hand _decorated_. Frackelton wrote in her book _Tried by Fire_ a century ago that "...transfers should not be sold for 'hand-work' as they generally and unscrupulously are ..." Nicola Monachesi reiterated this twenty years later in _A Manual for China Painters_ chapter titled "Decalcomania" — "When this method of decorating china is resorted to with the intent to deceive, it at once becomes an imposture that is very deplorable. The fact that many people are unable to detect the print from the painted decoration is rather an unworthy excuse for duping an unsuspecting patron by taking advantage of his ignorance." To this day it remains up to the individual to learn to discern the real from the impostor.

Photo courtesy of The McFaddin-Ward House, Beaumont, Texas

Figure 8
_Mineral colors came either in vials of powder that required grinding and mixing with a special oil or pre-mixed in tubes. Specialized brushes in a variety of widths and shapes were used to apply the strokes and background necessary to create paintings, patterns, and backgrounds._

Figure 9A

Figure 9B
*By the early part of the twentieth century, F. G. Coover was one of several companies offering thousands of outlined decal designs that could be fired onto porcelain. Then, china painters only needed to fill in the outlined areas with flat washes of color. Although these decals economized painting time, aesthetically they reduced china painting to a craft that required little artistic skill.*

Figure 10
*Sometimes pre-printed decals, such as the pansies on this plate, were enhanced with hand painted backgrounds. Commercial studios, such as The Buchanan Studio of Indianapolis identified on the back, wishing to save time and labor utilized this combination of decorating methods.*

*Porcelain pieces may be incorrectly identified as hand painted, rather than hand decorated. When viewed under a magnifying glass, decals, which are screen-printed, present a series of dots. Hand painted areas are either smooth or have visible brush strokes.*

# Chapter Three

## Identifying American Porcelain

Trying to identify and date American hand painted porcelain is a daunting task. Various obstacles are encountered in this process. At the top of the list is the fact that American china painters employed imported whiteware. Though certain styles and subjects remained indigenous to various countries and factories, sometimes there was overlap and "borrowing." Frequently, artists neglected to sign or date their finished pieces, and many continued to paint traditional subjects in traditional styles without regard for changing design trends. Further adding to the confusion, china painters and suppliers may have kept a stock of whiteware sitting upon shelves for years before they were decorated, making the use of factory backstamps an unreliable source for establishing dates. Despite these shortcomings, there are several approaches that can be implemented to assist one in solving the mystery.

### Differences Between European and American Porcelains

American porcelain artists painted on imported blanks.

Figure 11
*Flowers executed in the unique* deutsche Blumen, *or Dresden style were introduced at the Meissen Factory in Germany after 1730, and were copied by many factories located in nearby Dresden. This style of decoration remains in production today.*

This often has caused much confusion when it comes to categorizing where a piece of porcelain was decorated. Initially, a majority of whiteware came from Germany, France, and Austria. Porcelains from each of these countries feature a variety of styles that may be distinctive or similar to one another. Overall, however, their painting styles and motifs differ in many ways from American design. Therefore, it is essential to learn to distinguish between American and European paintings by looking for certain clues.

When Johann Friedrich Böttger first unraveled the

Figure 12
*The Sèvres Factory, located in France, gained a reputation for producing porcelains decorated with superb cherubs, offset by a solid ground color, as seen in this cup and saucer. Other motifs generated by this factory included courting couples, romantic landscapes, and florals.*

Figure 13
*Floral decoration from European factories in the nineteenth century often were brilliantly colored and photo-realistic. The plate on the left is Old Paris, ca. 1800 – 1830; the one on the right was manufactured and decorated by John Aynsley & Sons, England, 1887.*

process for manufacturing porcelain, the lack of artisans trained specifically to work with, and decorate, this new product, resulted in unimaginative creations. It wasn't until Böttger died in 1719 and Johann Gregor Höroldt took over as decorator for the Meissen factory that mineral colors were perfected and employed, and new kinds of painted decoration introduced. Under Höroldt's direction, chinoiserie designs, which were fanciful interpretations of Chinese culture, were employed, as well as Japanese Imari patterns and Kakiemon styles; red and black monochromatic paintings; armorial dinner services; landscape paintings; and flowers executed in the unique *deutsche Blumen,* or Dresden, style (Figure 11). In the mid-eighteenth century, when the Sèvres factory gained prominence, courting couples, romantic landscapes, florals, and cherubs, often framed by Rococo scrollwork and contrasted with a solid ground color, were in vogue (Figure 12). In the nineteenth century production of these motifs continued, with the addition of por-

Figure14A

Figure14B

*These three plates illustrate the stylistic differences between European and American painting. The plate at left in 14A is from a Limoges, France factory, ca. 1905, and is decorated in a quintessential impressionistic style. Adjacent to it is a typically English plate from John Aynsley & Sons, ca. 1910, where a realistic landscape is surrounded by a highly patterned border. The plate in 14B was decorated in the Chicago studio of A. Heidrich, ca. 1918-1922, and is more pictorial.*

traiture, game birds, fish, and landscapes as decorative motifs (Figure 13). These paintings were portrayed in styles ranging from photo-realistic to fanciful to impressionistic (Figure 14A and 14B).

In the United States, the ascent of the Aesthetic Movement was coincidental with the rise in popularity of china painting. Early china paintings were influenced by the writings and philosophy of the Englishman John Ruskin, one of the most famous leaders of the Aesthetic Movement. He and like-minded individuals believed that the greatest works of art drew inspiration directly from nature. Proponents of Aesthetic ideals suggested using natural sources for artistic inspiration. As a result, a more naturalistic style developed in the United States, one which depicted the individual variations and details of subjects. Flowers with turned petals and leaves with holes and tears were artistically rendered. Florals and fruits were the favored subjects of American china painters. It is rare to find American porcelains decorated with landscapes, Oriental patterns, or wildlife, as was common in Europe. Though cherubs were popular subjects in Victorian times, only the most ambitious and talented china painters attempted to paint them. Eventually, conventional and abstract designs gained equal ground, another style rarely seen on hand painted European porcelains. Despite subject limitation, American paintings offered more variety of style and composition because most were executed by independent artists rather than by factory-employed artists, evident in Figure 15.

### Figure 15
*By the turn of the century, over 20,000 Americans painted on porcelain, and their artistic styles and designs were as diverse as their numbers.*

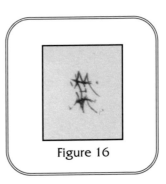

Figure 16

American porcelain paintings were often decorative in nature. Patterns were created and applied to enhance the utilitarian aspect of an object, unlike European porcelains which featured fine art works meant to exist on their own, separate from the function of the piece. Even when appropriate motifs were employed on European pieces, such as depicting fish on fish platters and plates, the paintings cover the entire surface. American dinnerware often featured border patterns that would have been chosen to compliment the kind of food served, such as a cluster of fruits on a jam jar. By limiting pattern to border bands, the decoration remained in view even when a plate was covered with food.

Many European decorated porcelains were unsigned because individuality was repressed in factory workshops. Some pieces may be discreetly initialed, signed with a surname, or marked with a decorator's insignia. Rarely are they dated. American painters who signed their work may have included their full name as well as a date. Others used only initials, or incorporated their initials into a stylistic cipher that may be difficult to read (Figure 16). China paintings completed before 1910 tend to have Spencerian-style letters and more florid signatures. Later on, artists used a block alphabet, or a more modern form of script. However, the lack of a signature — or the presence of one — on an American piece reflects little in terms of quality and pricing.

Throughout history most china painters, even when they autographed their artworks, remain undocumented and virtually unknown.

## Factory Marks and Origins

Factories used their own marks to identify their products, and these marks are useful in identifying when and where a piece of porcelain was manufactured. There are a myriad of books on marks that provide invaluable help when trying to date and identify the origin of porcelain (see Bibliography). If a piece of porcelain is identified with its country of origin, it was imported into the United States after 1890 when the McKinley Tarriff Law was enacted. If the words "made in" precede the country name, then the piece of porcelain was manufactured after 1914.

Since a particular mark may have been used for decades, marks are best limited to confirming a time period after first categorizing a porcelain by its decoration. *The country of origin and factory that manufactured the whiteware add no value to the final price of the porcelain.*

## Subject, Style, and Color

American porcelain decoration can be categorized by style,

Figure 17
*These two plates painted with wild rose motifs illustrate the differences between naturalistic and conventional styles. Naturalistic paintings were based on realism. Conventional designs simplified and reinterpreted natural forms within a geometric framework.*

color, and motif, which followed fashion trends of particular periods. As is often the case, trends overlap, making classification sometimes hazy. In general, during the latter quarter of the nineteenth century, a **naturalistic style** where subjects were portrayed realistically was predominant. During the mid-1880s a more abstract style began appearing in paintings. Known as **conventional style,** natural forms were simplified and interpreted within a geometric framework (Figure 17). Eventually, totally abstract patterns were also created. The chart below provides reference points for prevailing styles, and the colors and motifs characteristic of them.

---

## Styles, Movements, and Fashion Trends

**1875 – 1880**    **Aesthetic Movement** – Olive green was the most popular interior color, along with terra-cotta and ocher. Bronze powderings on walls and gilt in wallpaper and furniture were used as accents. In porcelain paintings, subjects were depicted in a realistic style that recorded natural quirks — a torn petal, a curled leaf edge. Violets, roses, and sunflowers were rendered in jewel tones of rich purples, rubies, and saturated yellows.

**1865 – 1885**    **Renaissance Revival** – In the dining room a richness of decoration was sought. Height and size were emphasized. China cabinets towered at seven to eight feet high. Carved sideboards stretched across entire walls. At this time, the walnut "hunt" sideboard became popular, with carved effigies of deer and hares, fish and fruit. Deep purples, violets, crimsons, and emerald greens were the favored colors, highlighted by gilding. Fruits depicted on porcelains were portrayed in an autumnal palette of russets, ochers, maroons, and warm greens.

**1880s – 1890s**    **French Style** – This style employed rococo curves and scrolls. Pastels, such as pale blue, ivory, light warm and cool greens, and soft pinks were used for delicate floral renderings, especially for baby rose and forget-me-not motifs that appeared in boudoir and parlor porcelain pieces.

**1872 – 1885**    **Eastlake Style** – Sunflowers, lilies, and poppies were favored floral motifs; roses were not. Peacocks, too, were popular. Eastlake-style designs were rendered in flat hues. Olive green was the preferred interior color, followed by ocher and terra cotta. Other popular color combinations included bronze-green and olive; terra-cotta and salmon; and olive green with peacock blue. Every surface was viewed as part of a continuous interlacing of two-dimensional pattern.

**1875 – 1880s**    **Anglo-Japanese Style** – The craze for things Japanese was interpreted in porcelain painting by asymmetrical and simple compositions carried out in soft and neutral hues.

**1880s**    **Exotic Revival** – Patterns were based on abstract designs from foreign cultures documented by Owen Jones. Intricate Islamic patterns were particularly emulated. It was during this time that conventional, i.e., geometric, designs developed in porcelain decoration.

**1890s – 1920s**    **Arts and Crafts Movement** – Moss green, maroon, and oatmeal created the preferred palette. Matte finishes became popular. Pattern disappeared from surfaces, replaced by flat areas of color, also in porcelain paintings, and the natural texture of materials.

**1890 – 1915**    **Art Nouveau Style** – Swirling patterns of stylized flowers, birds, and fruits were depicted in muted tones of green, lilac, and purple, as well as olive green, sage, and mustard.

**1900 – 1920**    **Colonial Revival Style** – During this time the trend for white and pastels, particularly rose and lavender, replaced the more brilliant hues of the previous century. Backgrounds were toned down with soft hues. Iridescence also became vogue, and mother-of-pearl luster was used with increasing frequency on porcelain surfaces.

**1915 – 1930s**    **Art Deco Style** – Shiny silver was contrasted with burnished gold in geometric patterns, often emphasized by black. Gold tones were combined with burnt orange, and pale blues, greens, and yellows. The use of iridescent lusters in porcelain decoration was more often employed.

**1930s – 1940s**    **The Depression and World War II** – Muted plums, cool greens, and beiges were punctuated by chartreuse, scarlet, magenta, and strong yellow. Typical color combinations of the 1930s included cocoa brown with hyacinth blue; dark purple with turquoise; and mustard yellow with gray. The 1940s brought in celadon and dusty rose, as well as kelly green paired with Chinese red.

Figure 18
*A naturalistic style developed in the United States which depicted the individual variations and details of subjects. Florals and fruits were favored motifs, portrayed in a painterly rather than graphic manner not generally seen in European porcelain decorations.*

A majority of paintings executed from approximately 1876 to 1900 reflect the ideals of Ruskin and the Aesthetic Movement. Labeled **naturalistic**, subjects were portrayed in an impressionistic manner with an appearance similar to watercolor paintings. Violets, forget-me-nots, daisies, and roses were the most popular floral motifs, followed by sunflowers and orchids. Within this period, an autumnal palette of russets, ochers, maroons, and warm greens was favored along with jewel tones of rich purples, rubies, and saturated yellows (Figure 18). Paintings depicting fruit on tableware complemented similar color schemes employed in most Victorian dining rooms. Pastels, such as pale blue, ivory, light warm and cool greens, and soft pink were appropriate for more delicate floral renderings of baby roses and forget-me-nots. Often these small-scale flowers adorned feminine articles. Such objects were used on dressing tables, and on serving pieces where tea would have been taken in the parlor, then a woman's bastion.

Charles Locke Eastlake, British author of *Hints on Household Taste*, was another leader of the Aesthetic Movement. His philosophy greatly differed from that of Ruskin, however. Eastlake felt that trompe l'oeil artistic attempts at realism were dishonest because they were nothing more than illusions. The writings of Eastlake echoed those of the English architect Owen Jones, who published *The Grammar of Ornament* in 1856. Jones's book

illustrated European ornament from prehistoric times up to the Renaissance. It also included motifs from Egypt, Assyria, Persia, and China. His writings, including *Plans, Elevations, Sections and Details of the Alhambra* which was published in 1842, as well as his drawings, became influential sources for American design.

Eastlake, like Jones, proposed that flat surfaces should be decorated with two-dimensional, geometrical designs, which became known as **conventional** style. Conventional designs were pure abstractions, though they could be derived from natural forms that were reduced to geometrical components. His ideas took longer to find acceptance in the design of porcelain patterns, but when they did gain ground, many artists adopted this approach. Conventional paintings were seen as "modern" in comparison to naturalistically-rendered subjects.

Turning their backs on the use of perspective and three-dimensional modeling, artists created flat, two-dimensional patterns for flat surfaces. Each component was outlined to emphasize its form; each enclosed shape was painted with a different color for further definition. For inspiration, they turned to the East and the Middle East whose cultures provided an enticing sense of mystery, and where archeological excavations unearthed material rich with artistic possibilities. Again, Jones's book *Plans, Elevations, Sections and Details of the Alhambra*, which was the

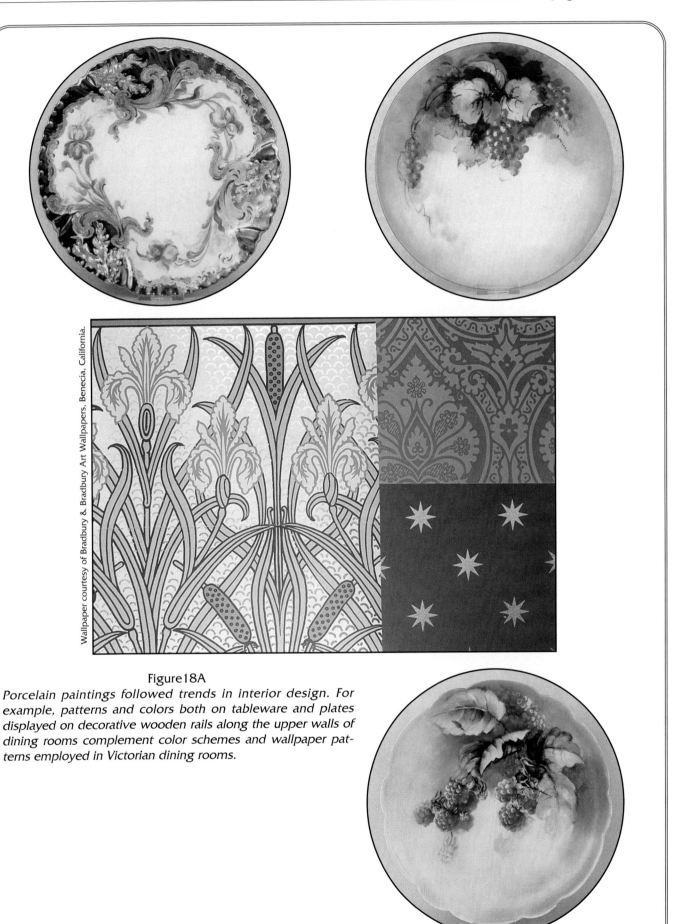

Wallpaper courtesy of Bradbury & Bradbury Art Wallpapers, Benecia, California.

Figure18A
*Porcelain paintings followed trends in interior design. For example, patterns and colors both on tableware and plates displayed on decorative wooden rails along the upper walls of dining rooms complement color schemes and wallpaper patterns employed in Victorian dining rooms.*

Figure 19
*Exotic motifs adapted from foreign cultures began gaining popularity in the mid-1880s. Porcelain artists looked to the East and Middle East for artistic inspiration. Islamic-style patterns, of which this plate is an example, were highly esteemed for their geometric designs and intricate interlacings.*

first systematic study of Moorish ornament at the Alhambra in Granada, Spain, proved influential (Figure 19).

Exotic motifs adapted from foreign cultures portrayed in a conventional manner, then, were the next style to gain ground. The stunning Japanese pavilion at the Centennial Exhibition launched a craze for Japanese culture. American artists and china painters were inspired by the flat, linear quality of their wood block prints and textiles, and by the simplicity and asymmetry of their designs (Figure 20). Concurrently, archeological finds in Greece, Egypt, and the Holy Land captured the imagination of many, as did the glamour of the Ottoman Empire, North African desert landscape, and Islamic culture. Forbidden from copying natural forms for religious reasons, Islamic patterns were highly esteemed for their geometric designs and intricate interlacings. Contrasting colors distinguished each shape within a pattern. In china painting, color was applied in washes that lacked tonal changes. Instead, design and pattern triumphed over naturalism.

In 1890 a new artistic trend crossed over from Europe, known as **Art Nouveau**. Natural sources were still employed for inspiration, but subjects were adapted as sinuous abstractions, as depicted in Figure 21. Artists concentrated on capturing and defining the essential, somewhat geometric, aspect of an object. They accomplished this by transforming drawings made from actual models into stylized motifs arranged in curvaceous compositions. Designs executed in the Art Nouveau style swirled and blossomed with an organic dynamism until 1915.

A revival of colonial architecture and neoclassical "white cities," i.e., classically-inspired designs reminiscent of ancient Greece and Rome but devoid of color, created at the Chicago (1893) and St. Louis (1904) World's Fairs sparked the trend for white and pastels — particularly rose and lavender — during the decades from 1900 to 1920 (Figure 22). Even compositions depicting richly-hued fruit had toned-down backgrounds in softer colors. Iridescence also became vogue, inspired by shimmering peacock feathers, butterfly wings, and ancient Roman glass.

As urban areas began to resemble cavern floors punctuated with skyscrapers rising like stalagmites, and the rhythm of urban life reverberated to an ever snappier beat, fashions in dress, art, architecture, and the decorative arts became linear and streamlined, with sharply defined silhouettes. Called the **Art Deco** style, it remained stylish from around 1915 well into the 1930s. The sinuous quality and recognizable floral forms of Art Nouveau designs were replaced by a straightened geometry containing totally

Figure 20
*The craze for Japanese style, which was inspired by the Centennial Exposition, was interpreted in porcelain painting by asymmetrical and simple compositions carried out in soft and neutral hues.*

abstract elements. Visual complexity often surrendered to simplicity, as portrayed on the porcelain objects pictured in Figure 23.

In the previous century the high gloss of glaze was considered gaudy by design standards and toned down with tints of ivory. In contrast, glitz was part of the Art Deco style period. Many porcelains from the latter part of this period retain an untinted ground. The use of shiny silver contrasting with burnished gold, initially borrowed from Japanese artistic sources, also reflects interior designs that combined the dramatic use of gold, silver, black, and white in imitation of glamorized movie sets. Other interior designers combined neutral tones of silver, gold, and brown with touches of pastel blue, green, yellow, and burnt orange. All these color combinations are evident in various conventional china patterns. Iridescent lusters were more commonly employed as well.

Many china paintings incorporated both naturalistic and conventional elements, echoing the psyche of a nation uncomfortable with completely releasing nineteenth century vestiges as it moved towards a future that changed shape with each new invention. There also remained china decorators who continued to employ a naturalistic style despite changes in artistic trends. Next to abstract, conventionalized paintings, however, their work began to look outdated.

Mary Louise McLaughlin wrote about naturalism versus conventional design in *The China Painters' Hand Book* (1917). In the chapter on design she stated that porcelain plaques meant to be hung upon a wall should be painted in a naturalistic style as an artist would paint a canvas. If the same plaque was to be inserted in a piece of furniture, she recommended instead a conventional design. Simplicity and suitability were guiding principles; paintings were not to interfere with the object's use or form. For example, a conventional border pattern was considered more appropriate for a plate than a central design which would be covered by food, as well as bear the brunt of use.

Echoing Eastlake and Jones, McLaughlin also wrote that conventional paintings were to be rendered in flat tints to harmonize with a piece of furniture's two-dimensional surface. This rule was incorporated by porcelain artists throughout the country who erroneously applied it to all sorts of three-dimensional objects, especially tableware. The most outstanding conventional designs which were executed in mineral colors either had complex patterns or simplistic patterns that were given interest with subtle modeling. Otherwise, the only flat-tinted decorations that were truly successful were those employing low-relief enamel. This style of decoration encompassed geometric interpretations of ancient patterns collected from various world cultures (Figure 24). It has sometimes been called

Figure 21
*Designs depicted in the Art Nouveau style often featured favored natural motifs transformed into stylized abstractions. Curvaceous compositions flowed with swirling visual rhythms. Muted tones of green, lilac, and purple, as well as olive green, sage, and mustard, were popular colors.*

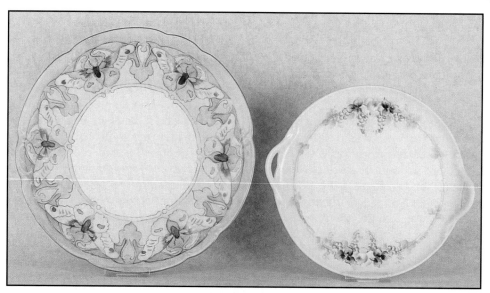

Figure 22
*Pastels were favored from 1900 to 1920, as seen in the soft hues of these plates.*

American Satsuma because of its similarity to Japanese Satsuma pottery, which also was decorated with colorful conventional florals and other motifs. Additionally, American china decorators employed Satsuma blanks for enamel work since its softer glaze was more suitable for this type of decoration.

Sensitively executed, conventional designs could be very sophisticated. Over time, changes in the china paint-

Figure 23
*Art Deco designs featured totally abstract, geometric patterns.*

Figure 24
*The most successful flat-tinted conventional designs were executed with low-relief enamels. This style of decoration encompassed geometric interpretations of ancient patterns collected from various world cultures, and has sometimes been called American Satsuma.*

Figure 25
*Porcelains decorated in the late 1930s and 1940s possess a simplicity and clarity that their Victorian predecessors lacked.*

ing industry spawned a general decline in quality. Some companies promoted the use of decal outlines which required merely filling in blank spaces with flat areas of color. Many artists directly copied designs from publications such as *The Art Amateur* and *Keramic Studio*, instead of using these as guides and samples. Designs became banal and execution suffered because there was less emphasis on technique and artistic training. Despite the present popularity of the Art Deco style, collectors must carefully discern quality level before investing in porcelains from this time period.

Eventually, the artistic pendulum swung in the opposite direction. Paintings from the late 1930s and 1940s once again turned towards nature as design source. The Depression of the '30s, followed by World War II, influenced a basic color palette that included muted plums, cool greens, beiges, and grays.

Typical color combinations of the 1930s include cocoa brown with hyacinth blue; dark purple with turquoise; and mustard yellow with gray. In the 1940s hopeful notes of clear, bright colors, such as chartreuse, scarlet, magenta, and strong yellow, colors borrowed from South America and the South Seas, occasionally punctuated the somber palette. Celadon was paired with dusty rose, kelly green with Chinese red. Combinations of bright, bold colors, such as cerise, scarlet, turquoise blue, apple green, and chartreuse were well-suited to fruit and floral compositions executed by china painters. Even when rendered naturalistically, designs were simplified. Whether realistically or fancifully rendered, paintings from this period possess a simplicity of design and a clarity that their Victorian predecessors lacked (Figure 25).

## Whiteware Forms

The type of articles painted and the shapes of porcelain pieces also need addressing. Plates ranked among the most popular of wares, and remain the most prevalent type of porcelain found in today's antique marketplace. Pitchers and cups and saucers were next in preference. Objects such as candlesticks and ring trees are more rare.

Some molds reflected the fashion for fancy shapes of the French style popular during the late Victorian era. Porcelains were rimmed with undulating and embossed edges, and handles were shaped by intersecting scrolls.

When neoclassicism and a colonial revival started the trend towards a more "modern" design in the late nineteenth and early twentieth centuries, many foreign manufacturers who catered to the American china painting market changed their molds in response. Rims were no longer dressed up with heavy embossing and undulating borders. Handles became angular and geometric. Consider, too, that conventional patterns would not have harmonized with rococo style china.

## Difficulties and Confusing Factors That Hinder Dating, and Clues That Provide Confirmation

It is dangerous to rely solely on backstamps when establishing the date of decoration. China painters and suppliers sometimes stocked porcelains for years before they were decorated. Then, too, paintings may incorporate aspects of various styles that make pinning down a date more difficult. The cup and saucer, pictured in Figure 26, is a case in point. Its backstamp identifies it as being manufac-

Figure 26
*Hecklin cup and saucer*

tured by Krautheim & Adelberg Porcelain Factory in Selb, Bavaria, circa 1884. Its sinuous border shows Art Nouveau influences, a style popular from 1890 to 1915. This porcelain was from a set of tableware identified as "Hecklin Studio, Minneapolis." Further research revealed that this studio was in existence only in 1916, placing the final date of decoration much later than manufacture, at the end of the stylistic period.

Sometimes clues found when perusing old magazines will confirm a backstamp. The plate decorated with a border of azaleas in Figure 27 has a Haviland & Co. backstamp that dates its manufacturing at 1891. A similar pattern was printed in *The Art Amateur* in the mid-1880s. It is safe to conclude, then, that this plate probably was decorated in the early 1890s by an artist who kept the magazine as a design reference in her art library. Likewise, the design and color application of the plate with a butterfly border was directly adapted from a design by A. F. Dalrymple published in the September 1908 edition of *Keramic Studio* (Figure 28A and 28B). The plate's Austrian backstamp was used from around 1910 to 1945. Based on the published

study, as well as the plate's ivory-tinted background, its decoration date places it between 1910 and 1915.

Comparisons between painted porcelains also are helpful when trying to lock in on a date of decoration. The plate on the left in Figure 29 has a Limoges backstamp that dates between 1879 and 1900. The plate on the right bears a German factory mark that was used between 1875 and 1935. Both backstamps include the country of origin, a requirement of the McKinley Tariff Law enacted in 1890. Therefore, it can be assumed that these porcelains were manufactured and decorated after 1890.

Subject, artistic style, and color palette also provide important clues, since paintings reflect color and fashion trends. At the turn of the century naturalistically rendered fruits were portrayed in autumnal colorations, as seen in Figure 29. The plates can be reasonably narrowed to having been painted between 1890 and as late as 1910, but probably not later. Interestingly, this time period gained additional credence when another piece of porcelain painted by the artist of the currant plate was acquired— a piece which the artist dated 1908.

Figure 27
*Azalea plate*

Contemporary porcelain artists usually paint on oriental and eastern European whiteware. These porcelains come with a paper sticker that is peeled off prior to firing. There is no permanent mark as on their European counterparts. However, in her book *Tried by Fire* (1885) Susan Frackelton recommended some manufactured porcelains that carried no backstamp, such as those from Gibus, and others whose marks burned away when a piece was fired. The lack of a factory mark, then, does not necessarily mean that a piece of porcelain is new.

Sometimes contemporary artists find or inherit old pieces of porcelain that they use as a canvas for their paintings. Factories also make new molds from actual antique forms. Even today, many porcelain artists do not date their work. Ultimately, the painting itself should provide the best identification clues, though anyone can be misled at times. By making comparisons, plausible conclusions can be deduced. Sometimes, it's a matter of luck and serendipity to find information that solves the identification puzzle.

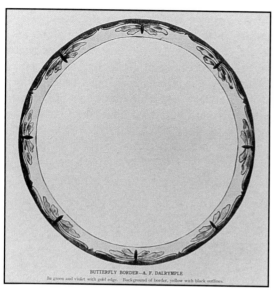

Figure 28A

Figure 28B

Figure 29
*Comparisons are helpful when trying to establish the dates of porcelain paintings.*

Figure 30A

Figure 30B

Figure 30C

Figure 30D

Figure 30

*These four porcelains illustrate how a natural motif, such as an iris, progresses from a naturalistic portrayal (A), to a stylized design (B,C), to one that is totally geometric (D).*

# Checklist for Identifying and Dating American Painted Porcelain

1. Are florals or fruits the main subject?

2. If the painting is naturalistic, does it depict individual variations and details in a painterly manner?

3. Is the design conventional, i.e., geometric and abstract?

4. Is there a signature or a date? Is the signature florid or in Spencerian-style script, likely dating the piece prior to 1910? Is the signature in block letters, indicating that the painting may have been completed after 1910?

5. Does the service plate or saucer have a border pattern, rather than a painting that encompasses its entire surface?

6. Is the color palette rich with saturated rubies, yellows, and ochers, consistent with fashion trends popular from 1876 to 1900?

7. Are pastels prevalent, dating pieces from about 1900 to 1930?

8. Is there an identifiable factory backstamp, usually from France, Germany, or Austria?

# Chapter Four

## Collecting American Painted Porcelain

### Determining Quality

Quality, and ultimately value, of American hand painted porcelain is determined by its decoration. Because so many American porcelain artists remain unknown, the artwork must be thoroughly evaluated. Successful paintings utilize the universal principles of design to organize various elements in a unifying way. They also exhibit a high level of technical skill and detail (Figure 31).

Figure 31
*The most successful porcelain paintings utilize the seven basic art principles: balance, contrast, dominance, proportion, rhythm, value, and variety, to organize various elements in a unifying way. These paintings also must exhibit good technique, which refers to the actual painting quality and artistic skill.*

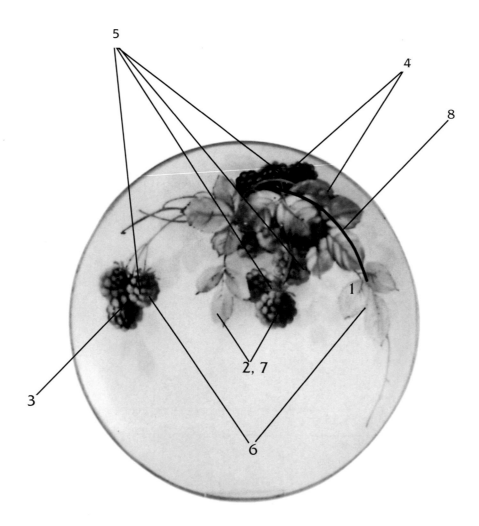

**1.** The soft blending of background color, clear detail, and smooth brush strokes are indicators of good **technique**.

**2.** Leaves are in **proportion** to the size of the fruit. Stems are thick enough to support the weight of the fruit and leaves.

**3.** This painting contains a full range of light to dark **values.** Contrasting values give the illusion of depth and dimension. They also define the center of interest.

**4. Contrast** occurs from differences in color and form. Deep purple contrasts with the yellow and yellow-red leaves, opposing colors on the color wheel, as well as with the cooler pale green and blue in the background. The roundness and smoothness of the berries contrast with the sharper edges of the leaves.

**5. Rhythm** is established by the repetition of color, line, and shape, providing various focal points that create a visual kinetic energy. **Dominance**, the interplay of focal points and

rest areas, is the basis of balance and rhythm.

**6. Balance** represents harmony and an equilibrium of elements. The three leaves on the right side visually balance the cluster of three berries on the left. Three green leaves to the left of the main cluster balance the three yellow-brown leaves to the right. The suggested symmetry of the design produces a calm effect.

**7. Variety** comes into play with differences in values and shapes, which provide visual interest.

**8. Line** refers to the dominant direction within a composition. In this painting the horizontal curve of the subject connotes gentleness and relaxed movement.

**Composition** is the design of a painting. It refers to the way colors, shapes, forms, and lines are organized. Artistic compositions encompass seven basic art principles: line, value, proportion, balance, rhythm, dominance, and contrast. Every design has these in varying degrees.

*Proportion* is the relation of parts to each other. Within a painting, a daisy should be larger than a forget-me-not. Flowers should have stems thick enough to support their weight. *Line* refers to the outlines of shapes, or the dominant direction within a composition. It expresses movement, as well as mood. *Value* represents the lightness or darkness of a hue. Most paintings have light, dark, and middle values. Used correctly, contrasting values give the illusion of depth, and define a focal point. *Rhythm* is the kinetic energy of a composition created by the repeated use of similar elements, such as color, line, or shape, that causes the eye to focus on different areas. The repetition of elements gives paintings a cohesiveness that pulls various elements together in a picture.

*Dominance*, or emphasis, is the interplay of focal points and rest areas. It comprises the basis of balance and rhythm. Most paintings have a center of interest, or focal point, which commands immediate attention. *Balance* represents harmony. Within every painting there must be variety and unity of various elements that create an equilibrium. *Variety* is the diversity of elements, i.e., differences in scale, line, value, and shape, that provides visual interest in a composition.

*Contrast* can be a difference of color, form or texture. Complimentary colors, i.e., colors opposite on the color wheel, such as violet and yellow, are contrasts. Clearly defined edges may contrast with edges that are softly blended into the background, forming focal points and rest areas. Brush strokes can be applied with a sweeping motion and blended to create a smooth, soft appearance in some places, while small and swift strokes produce a more patterned and energetic look in others.

Artists use light, shadow, and perspective to create spatial illusion. Within a painting, objects that are closer appear larger, and may hide or overlap distant objects. To foster a dimensional quality, paintings should have a distinct foreground, mid-ground and background.

**Technique** refers to the actual painting quality and artistic skill. Some artists have a bold style, making prominent brush strokes part of their artwork. This is acceptable. Sloppy strokes, blurred detail, or the lack of smooth blending are not. Great compositions and interesting subject portrayals can be destroyed by poor execution. Scrutinize carefully. Make sure subjects are botanically and anatomically correct. Nothing seems more odd than combining rose leaves with pansies, but some china painters have done just this!

Lastly, consider **originality**. Common subjects may be treated in an uncommon way — unusual color palette, subject portrayal, etc. — that brings a unique quality to an otherwise mundane painting. Be aware that many artists copied published studies. The painting you think is unusual and unique actually may have been adapted from magazines such as *Keramic Studio* or *The Art Amateur*.

---

## Quality Checklist

**1. Workmanship:**

Is the subject clearly defined?

Are brush strokes smooth?
Are backgrounds blended with smooth color transitions and no harsh edges?

Does the decoration have a slight sheen, indicating it was properly fired, or is the surface dull, meaning that the piece wasn't fired hot enough to fuse the paint with the glaze?

**2. Aesthetics:**

Is the detail sharp and clear?

Is the subject defined accurately?

Is the composition balanced and placed correctly on the object?

Is there a light to dark range of values and sense of perspective?

Is there a focal point?

Are the colors harmonious?

On conventional designs, is the outlining smooth, well-defined, and straight?

## Factors Affecting Pricing

Pricing porcelain is the result of a combination of subjective and objective judgments an antique dealer takes into consideration. Condition, age, rarity of whiteware and design, aesthetics (eye appeal), and size all affect the value of a piece of porcelain. Artistry, supply/demand, and geographic location also come into play. Ultimately, the beauty of a painting and the extent of the decoration outweighs almost any other element, except **condition**.

**Figure 32A**
*Despite the simplicity of design and the lack of a signature, the painting is professionally executed. Its value ranges between $18.00 and $25.00*

**Figure 32B**
*More detail means that the painting took longer to complete, and consequently, retains a higher value. This painting, which is more sophisticated that the plate pictured in figure 31A, is valued between $25.00 and $35.00. Note that the signature of an undocumented artist, as is the case here, adds little in terms of price.*

**Figure 32C**
*This plate, though not as sensitive to leaf details as the other two plates, is aesthetically the most appealing. Additionally, the use of gold scrolling makes it a more saleable item; therefore, it probably would be priced between $35.00 and $45.00*

*Factors Affecting Pricing*

Because of porcelain's inherent vulnerability, pieces in mint condition garner top dollar. Porcelain may not survive the years without some wear, however. Some porcelains with minor damage bear consideration, especially if the piece itself is rare or the painting exceptional. Then, too, pieces with noticeable damage can be restored. Remember that museums accept and restore many kinds of artwork, including porcelain, if the objects have value. Additionally, buying less than perfect pieces and restoring them may allow you to build a highly desirable collection at a more reasonable cost.

Mint condition means no chips, cracks, or flakes on the porcelain; no wear on the design or gilding; and no fading of colors. It is generally accepted that pieces with minor chips and a few light scratches retain a value 70 to 80 percent of a similar piece in mint condition. Where there is considerable wear, the value may drop by fifty to seventy-five percent.

**Rarity** covers the object itself. Common items, such as plates, cups and saucers, cost less than uncommon ones, such as sugar and creamer sets. Condensed milk containers, celery trays, and saltcellars are not only scarce but provide aspects of historical interest, e.g., when and why they were used, that may qualify a higher price tag. Additionally, since many porcelains broke over the years, the more complete a set, the more money it will cost.

Subject and color determine **eye appeal**, which, along with detail, calculate price. Illustrating these points are three plates painted with purple violets, pictured in Figure 32A, B, and C. All are in mint condition, similar in size, and decorated between 80 to 100 years ago. Equal in artistic quality, each one displays varying levels of detail.

The first one, which measures 7½" in diameter, is the simplest (Figure 32A). Despite the simplicity of design and the lack of a signature, the painting shows professional execution.
- The subject exhibits sharp detail and wide value range.
- Shadow shapes are used to fill out the composition and add soft contrast.
- The picture has a balanced, yet varied composition.
- Bold brush strokes show the hand of an experienced

and confident painter.

The second plate (Figure 32B), measuring 7¾" in diameter, has a slightly more elaborate edge and a more sophisticated layout. Here the painting exhibits the work of a delicate hand. Detail and value range are on par with the first plate. Shadow shapes fill out and add dimension to the floral clusters. The plate is signed "Harris," though nothing is known about the artist.

The third plate (Figure 32C) is the largest, measuring 8¼" in diameter. Like the first plate, its rim is simple and smooth, but an inner border has been dressed up with gold scrollwork. By far, this painting displays the greatest contrast and spontaneity in the brush work. In view of today's decorating trends, its cool color palette and design have the most eye appeal. However, the leaves are the weakest, and the painting lacks the sensitive rendering of the first two plates. It is signed "Luken," and was executed by the Chicago-based artist Minnie Luken.

The simplicity and size of the first plate places its value between $18.00 and $25.00. Because of the refined painting shown in the second plate, it would cost between $25.00 and $35.00. The third plate, though not painted with as much attention to detail as the second plate, is aesthetically more pleasing. Additionally, the use of gold scrolling makes it a more saleable item. Therefore, it probably would be priced between $35.00 and $45.00.

**Age** is a factor in pricing porcelain, but it is not the most important because pieces are not usually dated. In fact it is not uncommon to find contemporary porcelains costing more than antiques. In the porcelain marketplace, certain artists who have gained recognition and developed a following, demand and receive high prices.

Although signed pieces tend to add authenticity, from a valuation standpoint, **signatures** mean little unless the artist is documented. Well-known name brands, such as Lenox and Pickard China, always garner higher prices.

Gilding makes a porcelain object more saleable. However visually impressive, gilding requires little skill to apply in comparison to painting. In fact, an abundance of gilding should be a warning that a lot of gold may have been used to divert attention from poor painting technique. If all the

## Price Checklist

1. Condition
2. Rarity
    Is the object itself uncommon?
    Is the design or subject unusual?
    If the porcelain comprises a set, is it complete with no pieces missing?
3. Aesthetics, artistry, detail, eye appeal
    Does the painting exhibit technical excellence?
    Is there a lot of detail in the painting, making it more valuable?
4. Size
    Larger pieces of porcelain usually have greater value than smaller ones.
5. Age
    Generally, the older the porcelain, the greater its value. This isn't always true for the American market where dates may be difficult to verify, and a lot of painted pieces are less than 100 years old.
6. Signature
    Unless an artist or studio is documented and well known, signatures add little value.

gold were removed from any porcelain object — including one that was totally covered — there would be less than a dime's worth! Therefore, gilding adds only visual and not monetary value to the price of a piece of porcelain.

The quality of the artwork outweighs almost every other element. Good art commands respect. It abides by artistic principles, and displays professionalism in planning and execution. More detail means that a painting took longer to complete, and as a consequence, should cost more. American hand painted porcelain, a costly and time-consuming commodity to produce, will continue increasing in value as more people discover these one-of-a-kind treasures.

## Investing in Porcelain

The search for distinctive porcelains involves detective work, aesthetic awareness, and business acumen. Study, compare, and pay attention to detail. Personal observation is one of the best teaching tools. Don't make the mistake of entering the marketplace with inadequate knowledge. Read appropriate books and articles, and build up a library of basic references. Visit antique shops, antique shows, and museums. Comparison shopping is your best guide and a good way to build confidence. With time and experience, quality becomes recognizable. You will also develop a feel for realistic price ranges. Realize, too, that there are two other aspects that may determine value: these are what a buyer is willing to pay for a piece, and what a seller is willing to accept.

Establish goals to define the parameters of the collection you want to assemble. Your focus can be as broad as collecting pieces illustrating as many different flowers as you can find, or as narrow as obtaining only salt and pepper shakers. Collections are very personal investments. Buy what is appealing and affordable, and avoid impulse purchases. Remember that skillful buying is the key to building a good collection. Carefully examine pieces under consideration. Knowing when *not* to buy is as important as recognizing a good buy. Understand that tastes mature. When ready to upgrade, consider selling less desirable pieces to make room for new acquisitions.

Ultimately, the painting itself should be the major determining factor when considering the purchase of a piece of porcelain. Always ask yourself, "What will critics and experts think a hundred years from now?" If the painting is superb, the value of the artwork will remain.

---

### Sample Catalog Sheet

#96.04.07 (inventory number)

plate (type of object) *(Figure 33)*

8¼" diameter coupe (size and shape)

circa 1910 – 1920 (date of object and/or decoration)

two clusters of yellow and purple pansies break up a celadon green band outlined in black; pale green, pink, and yellow ground; burnished gold rim (description of decoration)

stamped in underglaze green "Gotham, Austria" (manufacturer and artist, if known; include sketches of backstamp and signature)

some gold wear in spots around rim (the condition of the piece)

porcelain manufactured by Fischer & Mieg and Oepiag and Epiag, Pirkenhammer, (1910) – 1945; see page 120 in Röntgen's *Marks on German, Bohemian and Austrian Porcelain* (references and remarks)

T. C. Antique Mall, West Palm Beach, Fla., April 6, 1996 (place and date of purchase)

$45.00 (value, including purchase price and true market value, if different)

---

## Cataloging Your Collection

Cataloging your porcelain collection is essential for insurance purposes, as well as for your own documentation. You can develop your own catalog sheets by following the format of accession records employed by museums and historical homes, or enter the data in a pre-bound record book. Creating a computerized database makes cross-referencing easy and is simpler to update when new information arises. Every entry should be illustrated with a photograph. Keep a file of receipts, or staple the receipt to the page.

Each piece of porcelain should be assigned an inventory number. This can be a numerical progression, or you can follow the format employed by museums. In their system, the first two digits of an inventory number represent the year of acquisition, and are followed by a decimal point. The next number is the number of the item purchased to date. If the porcelain is part of a set consisting of several items, the item number is then followed by another decimal point, and the number of items in the set are written out with commas in between. For example, if your fourth purchase made in 1995 was a 6-piece dresser set, its accession number would be 95.04.1,2,3,4,5,6. Each piece in the set would be identified individually as 95.04.1, 95.04.2, 95.04.3, etc.

---

**Tip:** There are two acceptable ways to mark porcelain. If you prefer to use an adhesive sticker, use #811 adhesive tape manufactured by the 3M Company only on an undecorated part, such as a base. Available in art and office supply stores, this adhesive comes in rolls, and is similar to the adhesive in Post-It ™ notes.

Another acceptable marking method consists of first brushing a layer of clear nail polish or other acrylic resin on an undecorated part of the base where you plan to write the inventory number. Let dry, and copy the catalog inventory number with a non-fading, light-resistant ink or acrylic paint; let dry. Cover the number with another layer of clear polish. Normal washing with water and mild detergent should not remove this information. Should you choose to sell an item, the number can be removed with nail polish remover (acetone), which will not harm the porcelain.

Figure 33
*Celadon pansy plate*
*(See description in Sample Catalog Sheet box, p. 46.)*

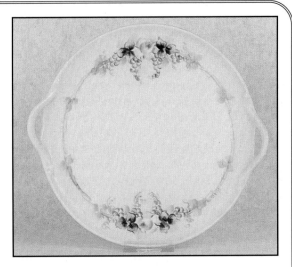

Figure 34A
*Steele cake plate*

Figure 34B
*Steele backstamp*

## Researching Your Collection

Most American china painters remain undocumented and unknown. Occasionally, if the artist or studio and city where they were located are marked on the porcelain, these may provide enough clues to start gathering more information.

Contact historical societies or libraries with archival departments that are located in the town or county where the artist practiced. You can find this information in the book *Directory of Historical Organizations in the United States and Canada*, edited by Mary Bray Wheeler (Nashville, Tenn.: American Association for State and Local History, 14th ed., 1990). Most libraries have this book in their reference section. Provide the historical society or library with as much information as you can, including approximate time period based on the piece of porcelain's factory backstamp.

Volunteers with these organizations will check city directories, censuses and other types of records. In this way you can find out when and where an artist worked. Most of the time the information can be obtained free, though you may want to make a small donation. Sometimes these societies are without volunteers or additional staff, and you may get no response. In this case, call them to inquire if there is a local genealogical society or historical researcher you can hire to check the information for you.

For example, the cake plate pictured in Figure 34A, which was acquired in 1992, is signed "M. E. Steele" and stamped "Steele Art Studio Spokane" (Figure 34B). The only other marking indicates that the porcelain was made in Germany. According to *Kovel's Know Your Antiques* by Ralph and Terry Kovel (New York: Crown Publishers, Inc., 1981), porcelains marked with the name of the country were probably made after 1891 when the United States government enacted laws requiring that the country of origin be identified, but before 1914 when the words "made in" were included along with the name of the country.

The Eastern Washington Genealogical Society in Spokane sent the following information: "The first listing for Mary E. Steele was in the 1896 city directory where she boarded with her father Joseph A. Steele in Hillyard, a northeastern suburb that was primarily the facilities of the Great Northern Railroad. Joseph was listed as general foreman, and continued in this capacity through 1918. Around 1899 the family moved to E. 801 Indiana." In 1900 Mary is listed as a telephone operator. From 1909 to 1920 she was listed with various china painting occupations. Therefore, based on the preceding information, we can surmise the cake plate probably was painted between 1909 and 1914. (Subject matter, style, and color palette are consistent with this time period, as well.)

I also received the names and occupations of her siblings, though there were no marriages recorded at the courthouse for any of the Steele children. Her family appeared to have lived together through 1918, and it's possible that Mary followed her family to Seattle after 1920. A search of the Washington state death indexes listed that her parents and one brother died in Seattle. Mary also died there at age 67 on September 28, 1941. Thus, we can determine she was born in 1873 or 1874.

The Curator of Special Collections of the Cheney Cowles Museum/Eastern Washington State Historical Society in Spokane wrote that in 1909 Mary E. Steele was listed in the Spokane City Directory as a china painting teacher boarding at E. 801 Indiana Avenue. In subsequent years, her occupation listed her as a china painter with a business address at 1025 Sprague Avenue. Later on, her business address changed to N. 811 Lincoln. Her last business address was given as S. 13 Post in 1920. One can speculate that Mary abandoned china painting in favor of more financially lucrative work, as did many artists.

A new resource with great potential has arisen from online computer database services. Via e-mail and electonic chat lines, people have the potential to reach relatives of china painters who practiced their art at the turn of the century. They may be able to gather information and documentation that would be difficult, if not impossible, to find otherwise, since surprisingly little was ever recorded.

Online services, have electronic bulletin boards for users to post messages. These computer services also offer user-friendly Internet access. Internet is the most popular international computer program, though using it requires the most patience because of its general scope. People can communicate through hundreds of newsgroup headings, posting messages, queries, and answers to one another. To find people who may have historical china painting information, it is necessary to take a hit-or-miss approach. The search can begin by identifying a handful of the newsgroup listings, using key words such as antiques, archives, art, craft, painting, or porcelain, that these people might read, though sometimes information may come from unexpected places.

A rapidly evolving arena is one composed of independent companies that specialize in servicing the antiques market. Some are available through the Internet, while others require their own software package. These companies offer additional benefits, such as illustrated buying and selling services, bookstores, calendar of antique-related events, directories, discussion areas, libraries, price guides, and auctions. Users can target exactly the information or task they desire without the guesswork involved in surfing the Internet.

As the new millennium approaches, we are witnessing a surge of interest in American painted porcelain from both a historical and collectible perspective. The history of the American china painting movement epitomizes the cultural, social, and economic upheaval that characterized the post-Industrial Revolution era. This once popular art form was part of a vast luxury consumer market, often neglected because porcelain's functional aspect has tended to override its aesthetic value.

Culturally, china painting encompassed Victorian arts and crafts ideals. (The Victorian era in America is defined by historians as the period between 1876 and 1915.) Central to this philosophy was the concept of turning one's home into an oasis with soothing colors, rich textures, and objects that implied something about the cultural cultivation of the occupants. One way to achieve this conversion was to turn everyday items into aesthetic masterpieces by employing hand-crafted methods. Hand painted porcelains allowed Americans to satisfy these principles, combining utility and beauty in a unique way.

Socially, a rising middle class with upper-class aspirations sought to emulate the wealthy, from their manners to their mansions. Porcelain represented affluence and tradition, connotations which appealed to those eager to display their social status and wealth with tangible assets. People appreciated the translucence, glimmer, and subtle richness that painted porcelains added to interiors and social events.

Economically, up until the latter half of the nineteenth century, porcelain was an expensive commodity, one that only the rich and royalty could afford. Technological advances during the Industrial Revolution made porcelain more available. Hand painted porcelains became vehicles, as well as status symbols of conspicuous consumption, that incorporated decorative arts into daily life.

Many porcelain artists painted only for themselves, their relatives, and close friends. Others sold their creations through studios, fine jewelry and department stores, art galleries, and art schools. As a result, many Americans came to adorn their mantels and tables with domestically-decorated porcelain rather than imported goods.

However, as the twentieth century progressed into its second decade, social and economic changes led to the eventual decline of the art form. Beginning around 1915, world events, technological advances, and economic and social factors infringed on the popularity of, and desire for, hand painted porcelains. Fashion-wise, Art Deco stylistic influences that crossed the Atlantic in the mid-teens created a demand for simplified, streamlined, and stylized designs. It became more difficult for porcelain artists to justify higher pricing, despite the precision required to execute favored abstract and geometric designs, and the inherent time-consuming nature of the medium. Additionally, as more women entered the workplace, they had less time to pursue hobbies that required as much time as did china painting.

It has been nearly a century since these heirlooms were created. Coupled with nostalgic decorating trends, we are bringing pieces out of china closets and finding uses for them. People are re-discovering the American painted porcelain treasures people cherished and prized for the artistry involved and the porcelain's remarkable properties.

# Chapter Five

## Photographs

All pieces pictured in this chapter were painted by American artists, even though porcelain backstamps are commonly of foreign origin. Because a backstamp says "Limoges," for example, does not mean the porcelain was decorated in France. Photos of porcelain decoration are arranged by subject and by style. Prices are inclusive of mint condition. Other factors, including age, rarity of whiteware and design, aesthetics and artistic quality, size, and geographic location also affect pricing. I have given realistic, average, retail value ranges. Bear in mind that there are times when a dealer has invested more than usual in a piece of porcelain because it may have been especially beautiful or rare. As a result, the porcelain will reflect a higher price tag than what is printed in this book. When this occurs, the dealer is counting on a buyer who will recognize the exceptional piece, and be willing to pay more to own it. Likewise, if there has been a slump in sales, a dealer may be willing to discount to move merchandise. Consequently, price ranges given here are meant to be used as guides, and therefore, are flexible.

Manufacturing dates are listed when the decoration is undated. Though some backstamps were used over several decades, based on the historical information contained in Chapter One, and the stylistic information in Chapter Three, it is safe to say that a majority of the porcelains pictured were painted prior to 1925.

## Naturalistic Style Florals

Front　　　　　　　　　　Back

Plate 1. *Syrup jug, 4"h. Overglaze paints, burnished gold handle, knob, and rims, and mother-of-pearl luster inside spout. Blank: ADK, France, ca. 1891 – 1910. Value:* ***$25.00 – 35.00***

Plate 2. *Cup and saucer. Overglaze paints, burnished gold rim and handle, mother-of-pearl luster inside cup. Blank: Germany, ca. 1891 – 1914. Value:* **$20.00 – 28.00**

Plate 3. *Cup and saucer. Overglaze paints, burnished gold rims, banding, and handle. From dinnerware set signed: Hecklin Studio, Minneapolis, ca. 1916. Blank: crown Krautheim, Selb, Bavaria. Value:* **$22.00 – 30.00**

Plate 4. Plate, 7½"d. Overglaze paints, burnished gold border and scrollwork. Blank: shield, Thomas Sèvres, Bavaria, ca. 1908. Value: **$20.00 – 30.00**

Plate 5. Cup and saucer. Overglaze paints, bronze rims, handle, and scrollwork. Blank: ADK, France; ca. 1891 – 1910. Value: **$22.00 – 30.00**

Plate 5A. *Bouillon cup and saucer. Overglaze paints, white enamel highlights, burnished gold rim, handles, scrollwork; Blank: T & V rectangle, Limoges, France, ca. 1892 – 1917. Value:* **$35.00 – 45.00**

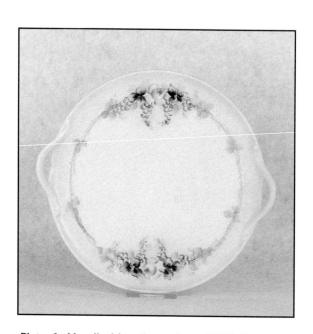

Plate 6. *Handled bon bon plate, 6½"d. Overglaze paints. Signed: M. E. Steele. Stamped: Steele Art Studio Spokane. Blank: Germany, ca. 1910 – 1914. Value:* **$15.00 – 22.00**

Plate 7. _Plate, 7¾"d. Overglaze paints, burnished gold rim. Blank: J & C, Louise, Bavaria, ca. 1902. Value:_ **_$18.00 – 25.00_**

Plate 8. _Plate, 7¾"d. Overglaze paints, burnished gold rim and detailing. Signed: Boerger, 1906. Blank: scepter, Silesia. Value:_ **_$20.00 – $30.00_**

Plate 9. *Plate, 6"d. Overglaze paints, burnished gold rim. Signed: M. Weislow. Blank: PM crown wreath, Bavaria, ca. 1904 – 1938. Value:* **$15.00 – $20.00**

Plate 10. *Vase, 7⅛"h. Overglaze paints, burnished gold rim. Blank: Belleek palette, Lenox, 1906 – 1924. Value:* **$250.00 – 300.00**

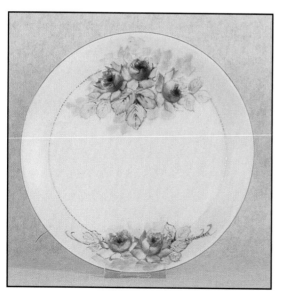

Plate 11. *Plate, 6"d. Overglaze paints, burnished gold rim and details. Signed: C. H. Nieburger. Blank: shield, Thomas, Bavaria, 1908+. Value:* **$10.00 – 18.00**

Plate 12. *Salt and pepper shakers, 3¾"h. Overglaze paints, burnished gold tops. Signed: L. Phillips. Blank: Royal wreath, O. & E.G., Austria, 1899 – 1918. Value:* **$20.00 – $30.00**

Plate 13. *Demitasse cup and saucer. Overglaze paints, burnished gold trim and scrollwork. Signed: KGP, 1900. Blank: France. Value:* ***$22.00 – 30.00***

Plate 14. *Dessert plate and tea strainer; plate 7"d., tea strainer, 6¼" w. Overglaze paints, burned gold rims, scrollwork, detailing, and monogram. Signed: L. V. C. Blank: plate, T & V rectangle, Limoges, France, Depose, ca. 1892 – 1917; tea strainer, none. Value:* ***$55.00 – 65.00***

Plate 15. *Saltcellar, 1¾"d. Overglaze paints, burnished gold rims, colored enamel jewels. Blank: none; ca. 1880 – 1915. Value:* **$20.00 – 28.00**

Plate 16. *Dessert set; plate, 6¼"d. Overglaze paints, burnished gold rims and handle. Signed: MacAllister. Blank: Japan, ca. 1925. Value:* **$30.00 – 40.00**

Front                                      Back

Plate 17. *Chocolate pot, 10"h. Overglaze paints, burnished gold handle and knob. Signed: M. H. Dorothy. Blank: GDA, France, ca. 1900 – 1941. Value:* **$125.00 – 175.00**

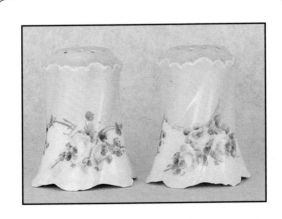

Plate 18. *Salt and pepper shakers, 2¾"h. Overglaze paints. Blank: crown, crossed scepters, Rosenthal Versaille(s), Bavaria, 1891 – 1907. Value:* **$20.00 – 30.00**

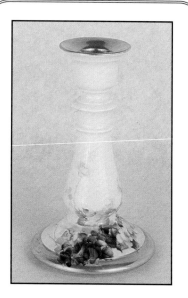

Plate 19. *Candlestick, 5½"h. Overglaze paints, burnished gold rims. Blank: France, ca. 1891 – 1914. Value:* **$45.00 – 55.00**

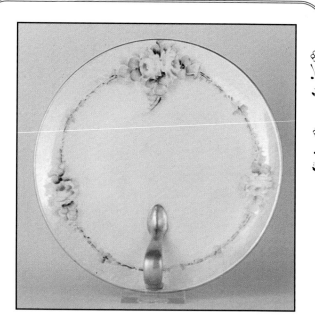

Plate 20. *Lemon dish, 6¼"d. Overglaze paints, burnished gold rim and handle, mother-of-pearl luster border. Signed: Gandy, 1925. Blank: none. Value:* **$22.00 – 30.00**

Plate 21. *Handled bon bon dish, 6⅝"d. Overglaze paints, burnished gold rim and handles. Blank: crown, crossed scepters, Rosenthal, Bavaria, ca. 1908 – 1920. Value:* **$35.00 – 45.00**

Plate 22. *Saltcellar, 1½"d. Overglaze paints, burnished gold rim. Blank: Belleek palette, Lenox, 1906 – 1924.* Value: ***$20.00 – 28.00***

Plate 23. *Lidded coffee pot, sugar, and creamer; coffee pot, 8"h. Overglaze paints, burnished gold rims, handles, feet, and knobs, white enamel embellishments. Blank: Favorite Bavaria, ca. 1908 – 1918.* Value: ***$175.00 – 250.00***

Front

Back

Plate 24. *Open sugar bowl, 4"h. Overglaze paints, burnished gold rim, handles, and feet. Signed: M. Perl. Blank: Favorite Bavaria, ca. 1908 – 1918. Value:* **$20.00 – 30.00**

Plate 25. *Plate, 6"d. Overglaze paints, burnished gold rim and border. Signed: M. Kaper. Blank: Hutschenreuther, Selb, Bavaria, 1887 – 1920. Value:* **$15.00 – 20.00**

Plate 26. *Plate, 6"d. Overglaze paints, burnished gold rim and borders. Signed: Luken (Minnie A. Luken, Luken Art Studios, Chicago, 1895 – 1926). Blank: UNO-IT, Favorite, Bavaria, ca. 1912 – 1918. Value:* **$10.00 – 18.00.**

Plate 27. *Lemon dish, 6"d. Overglaze paints, burnished gold border and handle. Blank: none; ca. 1918 – 1925. Value:* **$25.00 – 35.00**

Plate 28. *Lidded tea pot and sugar; tea pot 6¼"h. Overglaze paints, raised paste scrolls, burnished gold rims, borders, handles, knobs, and scrolls, colored enamel jewels. Signed: N.S.W. Blank: none; ca. 1880 – 1910. Value:* **$75.00 – 100.00**

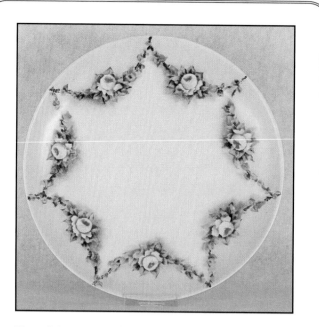

Plate 29. *Plate, 7¾"d. Overglaze paints. Blank:
crown, Krautheim, Selb, Bavaria, ca. 1884. Value:*
**$18.00 – 25.00**

Plate 30. *Oval dish, 8"w. Overglaze paints. Blank: PM crown wreath,
Bavaria, ca. 1904 – 1938. Value:* **$20.00 – 30.00**

Plate 31. _Cup and saucer. Overglaze paints, burnished gold rims, feet, and handle. Blank: cup, Limoges scroll, W. G. & Co., France, 1901; saucer, GDA, France, 1900 – 1941. Value:_ **_$22.00 – 30.00_**

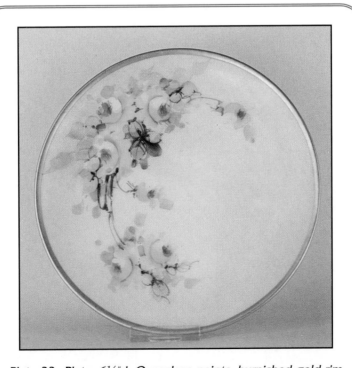

Plate 32. _Plate, 6½"d. Overglaze paints, burnished gold rim. Signed: Brown. Blank: shield, Thomas, Bavaria, ca. 1908. Value:_ **_$15.00 – 25.00_**

Plate 33. *Tiered serving tray, 13¼"h. Overglaze paints, burnished gold rims. Signed: S. W. Cartwright. Blank: horse and archer, Peerless, Bavaria, ca. 1935 – 1955. Value:* **$65.00 – 75.00**

Plate 34. *Lidded box, 5¼"sq., 3"h. Overglaze paints. Signed: WSO, 1913. Blank: D & Co., France. Value:* **$50.00 – 75.00**

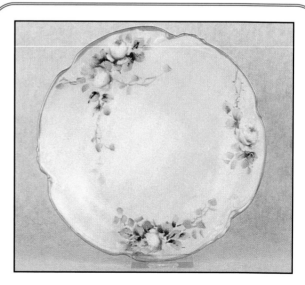

Plate 35. *Plate, 5¾"d. Overglaze paints, burnished gold rim. Signed: E.M.S. Blank: D & Co., France, 1879 – 1900. Value:* **$15.00 – 22.00**

Plate 36. *Sauce or bon bon dish, 4⅞"d., 2¼"h. Overglaze paints, burnished gold rim and feet. Signed: K.H.B., 1913. Blank: T & V rectangle, Limoges, France. Value:* **$45.00 – 55.00**

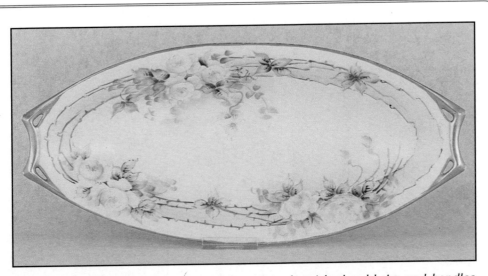

Plate 37. *Celery tray, 12"w. Overglaze paints, burnished gold rim and handles. Signed: Julia Hummel. Blank: Hutschenreuther Josephine, Bavaria, ca. 1887. Value:* **$35.00 – 45.00**

Plate 38. *Plate, 8½"d. Overglaze paints, burnished gold rim. Signed: F. H. Spear. Blank: R & Co., Limoges, France, ca. 1928. Value:* **$35.00 – 45.00**

Plate 39. *Plate, 6"d. Overglaze paints, burnished gold rim. Signed: Hackett. Blank: crown, crossed scepters, Gotham, Austria, ca. 1910 – 1920. Value:* **$15.00 – 22.00**

Plate 40. *Salt and pepper shakers, 3½"h. Overglaze paints, burnished gold tops. Blank: none; ca. 1900 – 1920. Value:* **$20.00 – 30.00**

Plate 41. *Vase, 6⅜"h. Overglaze paints, burnished gold rim and feet. Blank: crown, crossed scepters (Austria), ca. 1910 – 1925. Value:* **$50.00 – 60.00.**

Plate 42. *Calling card tray, 7⅞"w. Overglaze paints, burnished gold border. Signed: M. E. M. Blank: D & Co., France, 1879 – 1900. Value:* **$35.00 – 45.00.**

Plate 43. *Divided serving dish, 10"w. Overglaze paints, burnished gold rim, handle. Signed: I. S. Smith. Blank: B & Co., France, ca.1900 – 1914. Value:* **$65.00 – 85.00.**

Plate 44. *Plate, 7"d. Overglaze paints, burnished gold rim. Signed: Luneka. Stamped: G.H.B. Co., (George Borgfeld & Co., New York City, importer). Blank: J & C, Dayton, Bavaria, ca. 1902. Value:* ***$18.00 – 25.00.***

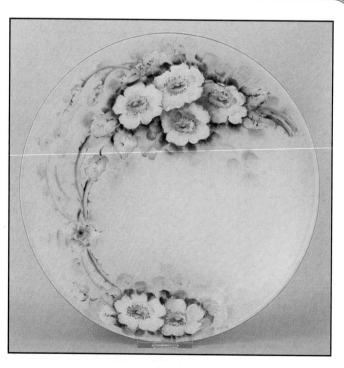

Plate 45. *Plate, 8⅜,"d. Overglaze paints, burnished gold rim. Signed: A. Held. Blank: shield, Thomas Sèvres, Bavaria, ca. 1908. Value:* ***$25.00 – 50.00.***

Plate 46. *Cake plate, 10¼"d. Overglaze paints, burnished gold rim, banding, and handles, white enamel embellishments. Blank: none; ca. 1890 – 1920. Value: **$45.00 – 55.00.***

Plate 47. *Handled sandwich or bon bon dish, 10¾"w. Overglaze paints, burnished gold rim and handle. Signed: Milne. Blank: Limoges scroll, W. G. & Co., Limoges, France, ca. 1901. Value: **$45.00 – 55.00.***

Plate 48. *Saltcellar, 2"d. Overglaze paints, burnished gold rim and feet. Blank: none; ca. 1890 – 1920. Value: **$20.00 – $28.00***

Plate 49. *Vase, 8½"h. Overglaze paints, burnished gold rim. Signed: J.P. Blank: Fraunfelter China, Ohio, 1925. Value:* **$35.00 – 45.00**

Plate 49A. *Plate, 7½"d. Overglaze paints, burnished gold rim, white enamel embellishments. Blank: bird, C. T., Altwasser, Germany, ca. 1909 – 1934. Signed: Lucy Miller. Value:* **$18.00 – 25.00**

Plate 50. *Master saltcellar or small bon bon, 2¾"d. Overglaze paints, raised paste, burnished gold border, scrollwork, and feet. Blank: T & V rectangle, Limoges, France, 1892 – 1917. Value:* **$22.00 – 30.00**

Plate 51. *Cup and saucer. Overglaze paints, burnished gold rims, handle, details. Signed: EM. Blank: Hutschenreuther, Bavaria, ca. 1887. Value:* **$22.00 – 30.00**

Plate 52. *Ring holder, 4½"w. Overglaze paints, burnished gold rim, hand, and scrollwork, white enamel embellishments. Blank: Royal wreath, O. & E.G., Austria, 1899 – 1918. Value:* **$35.00 – 45.00**

Plate 53. *Plate, 6"d. Overglaze paints, burnished gold rim and banding, white enamel embellishments. Signed: Luken (Minnie A. Luken, Luken Art Studios, Chicago, 1895 – 1926). Blank: UNO-IT, Favorite Bavaria, ca. 1912 – 1918. Value:* **$10.00 – 18.00**

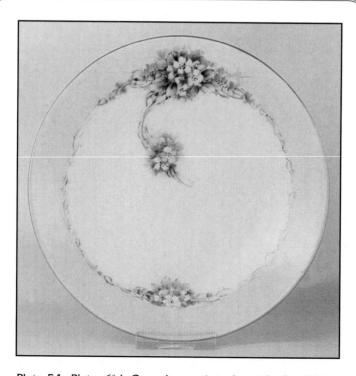

Plate 54. *Plate, 6"d. Overglaze paints, burnished gold rim. Signed: Baugh. Blank: crowned wreath, shield, PT, Bavaria, ca. 1903. Value:* **$15.00 – 22.00**

Plate 55. *Bon bon dish, 4¾"d. Overglaze paints, burnished gold handles, white enamel embellishments. Signed: A. J. Harris. Blank: none; ca. 1880 – 1910. Value:* ***$18.00 – 25.00***

Plate 56. *Butter pat, 2⅝"sq. Overglaze paints, burnished gold rim. Signed: E. Keller. Blank: H & Co., Haviland, France, ca. 1876 – 1879. Value:* ***$10.00 – 18.00***

Plate 57. *Tray, 12"w. Overglaze paints, burnished gold rim. Blank: T & V rectangle, ca. 1892 – 1917. Value:* ***$45.00 – 75.00***

Plate 58. *Powder box and dish; powder box 3¾"h, dish 6"d. Overglaze paints, burnished gold borders and handle, bright gold interior. Signed: M.O. Blank: powder box, Thomas shield, Bavaria, 1908+; dish, Limoges scroll, W. G. & Co., Limoges, France, 1901+. Value:* **$65.00 – 75.00**

Plate 59. *Punch or sherbet cup, 3⅛"h. Overglaze paints, burnished gold rim and foot, mother-of-pearl luster interior. Signed: M. Paddock. Blank: Epiag, Czechoslovakia, ca. 1920 – 1939. Value:* **$20.00 – 30.00**

Plate 60. *Cup and saucer. Overglaze paints, burnished gold borders and handle. Blank: T & V rectangle, Limoges, France, ca. 1892 – 1917. Value:* **$22.00 – 30.00**

Plate 61. *Plate, 6"d. Overglaze paints, burnished gold rim. Signed: McDonald. Blank: J & C, Bavaria, ca. 1902. Value:* **$10.00 – 18.00**

Plate 62. *Plate or saucer, 6"d. Overglaze paints, burnished gold rim and center. Stamped: illegible studio mark. Blank: J.P.L., France, ca. 1906. Value:* **$15.00 – 22.00**

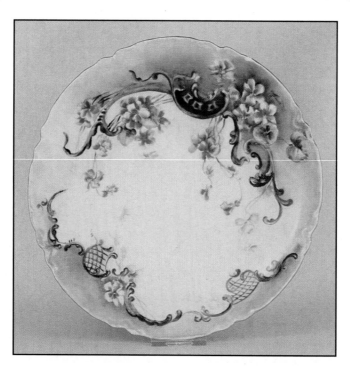

Plate 63. *Plate, 8½"d. Overglaze paints, burnished gold rim. Blank: H & Co., Haviland, France, ca. 1888 – 1896. Value:* **$35.00 – 45.00**

Plate 64. *Cup and saucer. Overglaze paints, burnished gold rims, banding, and handle, white enamel embellishments. Blank: none, ca. 1900 – 1920. Value:* **$15.00 – 22.00**

Plate 65. *Plate, 7¾"d. Overglaze paints, burnished gold rim, white enamel embellishments. Signed: Harris. Blank: crown, crossed scepters, Rosenthal, Bavaria, 1891 – 1907. Value:* **$25.00 – 35.00**

Plate 66. *Cake plate, 10"d. Overglaze paints, burnished gold rim and handles. Signed: Hall. Stamped: Gaine's Studio, Akron, Ohio. Blank: crown, crossed scepters, Rosenthal, Selb-Bavaria, 1908 – 1953. Value:* **$45.00 – 55.00**

Plate 67. *Plate, 7½"d. Overglaze paints, burnished gold rim. Blank: T & V, Thomas Sèvres, Bavaria, ca. 1908. Value:* **$18.00 – 25.00**

Plate 68. _Saucer, 5⅜"d. Overglaze paints, burnished gold rim. Blank: Haviland, France, ca. 1894 – 1931. Value:_ **_$10.00 – 18.00_**

Plate 69. _Plate, 8¼"d. Overglaze paints, burnished gold rim and scrollwork, white enamel embellishments. Signed: Luken (Minnie A. Luken, Luken Art Studios, Chicago, 1895 – 1926). Blank: Favorite Bavaria, ca. 1908 – 1918. Value:_ **_$35.00 – 45.00_**

Plate 70A

Plate 70

Plate 70B

Plate 70C

Plate 70D

Plate 70 A, B, C, D. *Master berry bowl, 3 serving bowls; master bowl, 9"d, serving bowls, 6⅝"d. Overglaze paints, burnished gold borders. Signed: H.B.F. Blank: master bowl, T & V rectangle, ca. 1892 – 1917; serving bowls, CFH/GDM, 1870 – 1882.* Value: **$125.00 – 175.00**

Plate 71. *Plate, 7½"d. Overglaze paints, burnished gold rim. Stamped: George H. Bowman & Co., Cleveland, Ohio (importer). Blank: J & C, Dayton, Bavaria, ca. 1902. Value:* ***$20.00 – 30.00***

Plate 72. *Handled bon bon plate, 7"d. Overglaze paints, burnished gold rim and handles. Signed: TMR. Blank: Germany, ca. 1891 – 1914. Value:* ***$20.00 – 30.00***

Plate 73. *Plate, 7½"d. Overglaze paints, burnished gold rim. Signed: WANDS (William D. Wands, Chicago, 1910 – 1916). Blank: Favorite Bavaria, ca. 1908 – 1918. Value:* **$18.00 – 25.00**

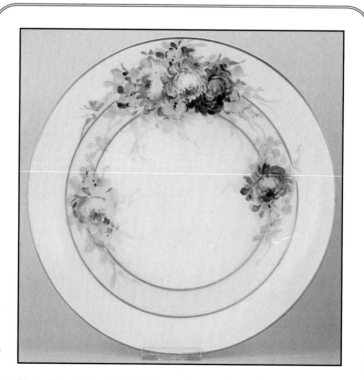

Plate 74. *Plate, 8⅜"d. Overglaze paints, burnished gold rim and banding. Signed: Kreis (Carrie S. Kreis, Marion, Ohio, ca. 1901 – 1918). Blank: crown, H & Co., Bavaria, ca. 1911 – 1934. Value:* **$25.00 – 35.00**

Front

Back

Plate 74A. _Gravy boat, 2⅝"h. Overglaze paints, burnished gold rim. Signed: (illegible). Blank: none; ca. 1880 – 1915. Value:_ **_$35.00 – 50.00_**

Plate 75. _Plate, 8¼"d. Overglaze paints, burnished gold rim. Blank: crown, crossed scepters, Gotham, Austria, ca. 1910 – 1945. Value:_ **_$25.00 – 35.00_**

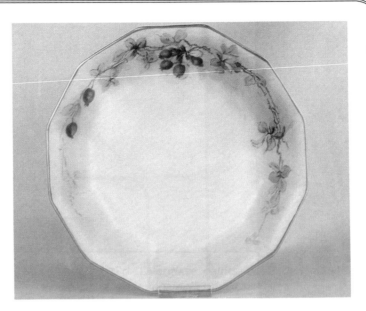

Plate 99. *Bowl, 7⅝"d. Overglaze paints, burnished gold rim. Blank: star Limoges, France, 1891 – 1914. Value:* ***$20.00 – 30.00***

Plate 100. *Plate, 6⅞"d. Overglaze paints, burnished gold rim. Blank: J & C, Bavaria, ca. 1902. Value:* ***$18.00 – 25.00***

Plate 128. _Baby cup, 4"h. Overglaze paints, burnished gold rim and handle. Blank: none. Ca. 1915 – 1920. Value:_ **_$18.00 – 25.00_**

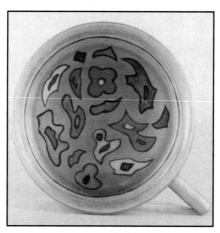

Plate 129. Cup and saucer. Overglaze paints, burnished gold borders and handle, mother-of-pearl luster interior of cup and base of saucer. Signed: F. H. Gordon, 1925. Blank: H & Co. Value: **$22.00 – 30.00**

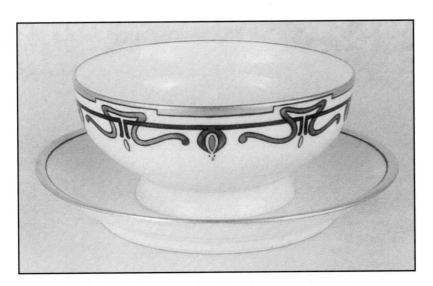

Plate 130. *Mayonnaise dish, attached underplate, 5⅝"d, 2¼"h. Overglaze paints, burnished gold borders, colored enamel details. Signed: E. H. Hall. Blank: Haviland, France, ca. 1894 – 1931. Value:* **$18.00 – 25.00**

Plate 131. *Mustard set; lidded pot, 3½"h; spoon; underplate, 5½"d. Overglaze paints, burnished gold rims, handles, and borders. Signed: E.L.H. Blank: wreath, scepter, RS, Germany, ca. 1904 – 1938. Value:* **$45.00 – 55.00**

Plate 132. *Plate, 8½"d. Overglaze paints, burnished gold rim and borders. Signed: P.N.C. Blank: crown and scepter, Silesia, ca. 1930 – 1940. Value:* **$25.00 – 35.00**

Plate 133. *Plate, 9¼"d. Overglaze paints. Blank: bird, C.T., Germany, ca. 1934. Value:* **$45.00 – 55.00**

Plate 133A. _Fruit bowl, 10"d. Overglaze paints, burnished gold. Signed: Louise M. Pflaum. Blank: crown and scepter, Silesia, ca. 1883 – 1930. Value:_ **_$60.00 – 80.00_**

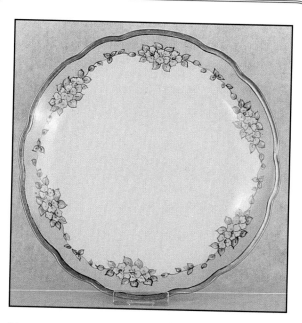

Plate 148A. *Plate, 7½"d. Overglaze paints, burnished gold rim. Signed: R. W. Z. Blank: bird, Austria, ca. 1884 – 1909. Value:* **$18.00 – 25.00**

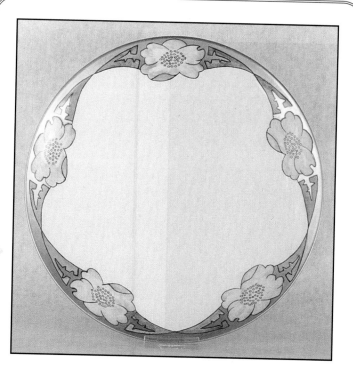

Plate 149. *Plate, 8¾"d. Overglaze paints, burnished gold rim. Signed: Evelyn Locke, 1931. Blank: arm with sword, Epiag Ivory, Czechoslovakia. Value:* **$25.00 – 35.00**

Plate 150. *Trivet, 6¼"d. Overglaze paints, burnished gold border, mother-of-pearl luster. Stamped: illegible. Blank: none, ca. 1918 – 1930. Value:* **$25.00 – 35.00**

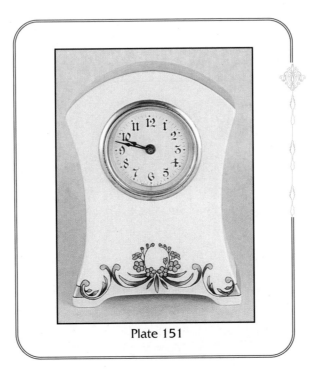

Plate 151

Plate 151. *Dresser set: tray, powder box, hair receiver, dresser box, hairpin box, clock; tray, 11"w. Overglaze paints, burnished gold banding, rims, feet, knobs. Signed: B.J.S., 1924. Blank: various manufacturers from France, Austria, and Czechoslovakia. (See close-up of pieces above and on next page.)* Value: **$300.00 – 375.00**

Plate 151

Plate 151

Plate 152. _Creamer, 3¼"h. Overglaze paints, burnished gold rim, handle, and outlining. Signed: W. Wilson. Blank: France, ca. 1891 – 1914. Value:_ **_$20.00 – 30.00_**

Plate 153. _Dessert set; plate, 7¾"d. Overglaze paints, burnished gold rims and handle. Signed: Mrs. P. B. Simmons. Blank: plate, shield, Thomas Sèvres, Bavaria, ca. 1908; cup and saucer, Haviland, France, 1893 – 1930. Value:_ **_$30.00 – 40.00_**

Plate 154. *Jardiniere, 5½"h. Colored enamel, burnished gold rim, border and feet. Signed: Clara M. Smith, January 1928. Blank: Belleek palette, Lenox. Value:* **$65.00 – 115.00**

Plate 155. *Jardiniere, 10¾"h. Overglaze paints, burnished gold. Signed: Clara M. Smith, April 14, 1925. Blank: crown, H & Co., Selb, Bavaria. Value:* **$275.00 – 375.00**

# Chapter Six

## Tools of the Trade

What tools do serious collectors need? There really are only three things anyone requires when seeking American hand painted porcelain: a magnifying glass, a reference library, and one's own good sense of design. A magnifying glass, or jeweler's loupe, is necessary to look at fine detail not to only check quality, but also to discern whether a piece of porcelain is painted or decorated with a decal. Decals are multi-colored pictures that have been screen-printed onto a paper or plastic sheet. Like overglaze painting, decals also must be fired on to become permanent. However, because decals are mass-produced, porcelains decorated with these usually are not as valuable as hand painted pieces.

For the most benefit, use a magnifying glass or loupe with at least ten times (10x) magnification power. The screen-printing process produces an all-over pattern of dots that become apparent when viewed under a magnifying lens. Hand painted pieces show evidence of brush strokes.

A basic reference library is essential for education purposes, as well as to identify factory marks. Two of the best books on antiques are *Kovels' Know Your Antiques* by Ralph and Terry Kovel (Crown publishers, Inc., 1981), and *Emyl Jenkins' Appraisal Book* by Emyl Jenkins (Crown Publishers, Inc., 1989). In Kovels' book, the section on pottery and porcelain gives an excellent and easy-to-follow, step-by-step approach for evaluating a piece of porcelain, one they dubbed "the Instant Expert." The authors also discuss various factories, countries, and types of pottery in-depth, providing readers with a general overview. The subtitle to Emyl Jenkins' book sums up her approach: "Identifying, Understanding, and Valuing Your Treasures." She discusses antiques from an insurance standpoint, details a system of cataloging and appraising your collection, and includes a section on china.

There are numerous books on factory backstamps, many of which are good. For American-decorated porcelain, the most helpful and accurate references include *Dictionary of Marks – Pottery and Porcelain* by Ralph M. and Terry H. Kovel (Crown Publishers, Inc., 1953); *Kovels' New Dictionary of Marks* by the same authors (Crown Publishers, Inc., 1986); *Marks on German, Bohemian and Austrian Porcelain: 1710 to the Present* by Robert E. Röntgen (Schiffer Publishing Ltd., 1981); and *Handbook of Pottery & Porcelain Marks* by J. P. Cushion, in collaboration with W. B. Honey, 4th edition (Faber and Faber, 1980).

Those who are especially serious about scholarship need to review old catalogs from porcelain importers, such as Thayer & Chandler, Burley & Tyrell, and Pitkin & Brooks, to name a few. Catalogs such as these provide invaluable information about the possible uses for the various blanks. They also show the pieces that constitute complete sets, including dresser sets, breakfast sets, lemonade sets, celery sets, etc. Old art magazines, including *The China Decorator* (1887 – 1901), *The Art Amateur* (1879 – ca.1903), and *Keramic Studio* (1899 – 1929), are filled with patterns that assist with the identification and dating of similarly decorated porcelains. Other magazines, such as *Ladies' Home Journal,* which also periodically printed articles on china designs, more importantly provide crucial lifestyle and home decorating information.

Confidence and knowledge are gained by many hours of reading and time spent comparing all types of porcelain. There are no short cuts. Because painting styles can be copied, the more porcelain viewed — in museums, at antique shops and flea markets, even in other people's homes — the more essential skills are gained. Over time, the origin and time-frame of decorated porcelain will become apparent, as well as the ability to discriminate the best from the mediocre, the unusual from the mundane. Above all, no matter when, where, or by whom a piece of porcelain was painted, quality — and ultimately value — is determined most by a painting's excellence.

# Glossary

**abstract:** An artistic style where forms and colors are reduced to basic geometric components, often bearing little resemblance to recognizable models.

**Aesthetic Movement:** A movement that lasted from about 1876 to 1900 that put into practice John Ruskin's ideas. These included using natural sources for artistic inspiration, rendered in a three-dimensional, naturalistic style, and turning everyday objects into beautiful artworks.

**Art Deco:** Characterized by pure geometry, this artistic style followed Art Nouveau and also originated in Europe. It was popular in America from the mid-teens to well into the 1930s.

**Art Nouveau:** An artistic style that originated in Europe and was popular in the United States from about 1890 to 1915. Art Nouveau designs are stylized abstractions of organic forms, usually of flowers and leaves, characterized by sinuous, flowing lines, curves, and shapes.

**Arts and Crafts Movement:** Charles Locke Eastlake was another leader of the Aesthetic Movement, but one whose ideas differed greatly from Ruskin. Eastlake felt that attempts to copy nature were merely poor illusions of the real thing. Flat, geometrical, conventionalized patterns characterize designs executed in this style. The resulting movement became known as the Arts and Crafts Movement in America. The Eastlake style, popular from around 1872 to 1885, evolved into the Arts and Crafts style in the 1890s, one which lasted into the 1920s.

**backstamp:** The porcelain manufacturer's mark, usually located on the base of a piece, identifying the factory, its location, and time period during which a piece of porcelain was made. Also called a mark.

**Belleek:** This type of ceramic is made from similar ingredients as hard-paste porcelain, and shares characteristics of translucency and vitreosity. However, unlike true porcelain, Belleek's lustrous pearl glaze never unifies with the clay body. Because Belleek becomes vitreous in the first firing, the glaze cannot permeate the body, and instead envelops it.

**biscuit/bisque:** Unglazed porcelain which has been fired to harden the clay body.

**blanks:** Undecorated, glazed white porcelain. Also called whiteware.

**bone china:** A mixture of china clay and china stone to which bone ash has been added for strength and whiteness.

**burnish:** To polish Roman gold after firing in order to bring out a soft sheen.

**china:** Another name for porcelain, originally applied to porcelain imported from China. Also means dinnerware made from various vitrified clay bodies.

**china clay:** A white clay that forms when rocks containing feldspar (aluminum silicate) decompose through weathering. Also known as kaolin, one of two basic ingredients of hard-paste porcelain.

**china painting/china decorating:** The fine art of decorating porcelain with various paints, metals, enamels, etc.

**china stone:** Another term for petuntse, which is a feldspathic rock, and one of two basic ingredients of hard-paste porcelain.

**chinoiserie:** An artistic and fanciful interpretation depicting the exotic world of Chinese culture. This style, which was peculiar to Europe, was developed in the eighteenth century.

# Bibliography

## Books

*American Art Pottery*. New York: Cooper-Hewitt Museum (The Smithsonian Institution), 1987.

Atterbury, Paul, gen. ed. *The History of Porcelain*. New York: William Morrow and Company, Inc., 1982.

Banham, Joanna, Julia Porter, and Sally Macdonald. *Victorian Interior Style*. London: Studio Editions Ltd., 1995.

Barber, Edwin AtLee. *Marks of American Potters*. Philadelphia: Patterson & White, 1904.

_____. *Pottery and Porcelain of the United States*. Watkins Glen, N.Y.: Century House Americana, 1971.

Battie, David, gen. ed. *Sotheby's Concise Encyclopedia of Porcelain*. Boston: Little, Brown and Company, 1990.

Berges, Ruth. *From Gold to Porcelain: The Art of Porcelain and Faience*. New York: Thomas Yoseloff, 1963.

Boger, Louise Ade. *The Dictionary of World Pottery and Porcelain: From Prehistoric Times to the Present*. New York: Charles Scribner's Sons, 1971.

Burton, William. *A General History of Porcelain*, Vol. I & II. London: Cassell and Company, Ltd., 1921.

Cameron, Elisabeth. *Encyclopedia of Pottery & Porcelain: The 19th & 20th Centuries*. London: Faber and Faber, 1986.

Chaffer, William. *Collector's Handbook of Marks and Monograms on Pottery and Porcelain*. Alhambra, Calif. Borden Publishing Company [n.d.]

_____. *Marks & Monograms on European and Oriental Pottery & Porcelain*. Alhambra, Calif.: Borden: Publishing Company, [n.d.]

Charleston, Robert J., ed. *World Ceramics*. London: Paul Hamlyn, 1968.

Chefetz, Sheila. *Antiques for the Table*. Text by Alexandra Enders. Viking Studio Books. NY: Penguin Books USA Inc., 1993.

Clark, Garth. *American Ceramics 1876 to Present*. New York: Abbeville Press, 1987.

Cooper, Emmanuel. *A History of World Pottery*, 2nd rev. ed. New York: Larousse & Co. Inc., 1981.

Cox, Warren E. *The Book of Pottery and Porcelain*, Vol. I & II. New York: Crown Publishers, 1944.

Cushion, John. *Pottery & Porcelain*. New York: Hearst Books, 1972.

Darling, Sharon S. *Chicago Ceramics & Glass: An Illustrated History from 1871 to 1933*. Chicago: Chicago Historical Society, 1979.

Dean, Patricia, ed. *The Official Guide to Pottery & Porcelain*. Orlando, Fla.: Thomas E. Hudgeons III, The House of Collectibles, Inc., 1984.

Delehanty, Randolph. *In the Victorian Style*. San Francisco: Chronicle Books, 1991.

Donhauser, Paul S. *History of American Ceramics: The Studio Potter*. Dubuque, Iowa: Kendall/Hunt Publishing Company, 1978.

Duncan, Alastair. *Treasures of the American Arts and Crafts Movement: 1890 – 1920*. New York: Harry N. Abrams, Inc., 1988.

Durdik, Jan,; Dagmar Hejdova; et. al. *The Pictorial Encyclopedia of Antiques*. London: The Hamlyn Publishing Group Ltd., 1971.

Eastlake, Charles L. *Hints on Household Taste*. Intro. John Gloag. New York: Dover Publications, Inc., 1969.

*Eighteenth to Twentieth Century American Porcelain*. Chicago: The Art Institute of Chicago, 1967.

Evans, Paul. *Art Pottery of the United States*. New York: Charles Scribner's Sons, 1974.

Feck, Luke. *Yesterday's Cincinnati*. Miami: E. A. Seeman Publishing, Inc., 1975.

Feild, Rachael. *MacDonald Guide to Buying Antique Pottery & Porcelain*. Radnor, Pa.: Wallace-Homestead Book Company, 1987.

Frelinghuysen, Alice Cooney. *American Porcelain: 1770 – 1920*. Distrib. Harry N. Abrams, Inc. New York: The Metropolitan Museum of Art, 1989.

Gaston, Mary Frank. *The Collector's Encyclopedia of Limoges Porcelain*. 2nd rev. ed. Paducah, Ky.: Collector Books, 1992.

Haggar, Reginald G. *The Concise Encyclopedia of Continental Pottery & Porcelain*. New York: Hawthorn Books, Inc., 1960.

Hughes, G. Bernard. *Victorian Pottery and Porcelain*. London: Country Life Limited, 1959.

Jacobson, Gertrude Tatnall. *Haviland China: Vol. I and II*. Des Moines: Wallace-Homestead Book Co., 1979.

Jenkins, Emyl. *Emyl Jenkins' Appraisal Book*. New York: Crown Publishers, Inc., 1989.

Kaplan, Wendy. *"The Art that is Life": The Arts & Crafts Movement in America, 1875 – 1920*. Boston: Little, Brown and Company, and Museum of Fine Arts, 1987.

Ketchum, Jr., William C. *The Knopf Collectors' Guides to American Antiques: Pottery & Porcelain*. New York: Alfred A. Knopf,

A Chanticleer Press Edition, 1983.

Kovel, Ralph M. and Terry. *Dictionary of Marks – Pottery and Porcelain.* New York: Crown Publishers, Inc., 1953.

_____. *The Kovels' Collector's Guide to American Art Pottery.* New York: Crown Publishers, Inc., 1974

_____. *Kovel's New Dictionary of Marks.* New York: Crown Publishers, Inc., 1986.

_____. *Kovel's Know Your Antiques.* Rev. ed. New York: Crown Publishers, Inc., 1981.

*The Ladies, God Bless 'Em: The Women's Art Movement in the Nineteenth Century.* (Exhibition Catalog.) Cincinnati: Cincinnati Art Museum, 1976.

Lehner, Lois. *Lehner's Encyclopedia of U.S. Marks on Pottery, Porcelain & Clay.* Paducah, Ky.: Collector Books, 1988.

Leopold, Allison Kyle. *Victorian Splendor.* New York: Stewart, Tabori and Chang, 1986.

Levin, Elaine. *The History of American Ceramics: 1607 to the Present.* New York: Harry N. Abrams, Inc., 1988.

Little, Ruth. *Painting for Pleasure and Profit.* Lubbock, Tex.: Brack Publications, 1963.

Marryat, Joseph, pub. *A History of Pottery and Porcelain,* 3rd ed. London: John Murry, 1868.

McClinton, Katharine Morrison. *Collecting American Victorian Antiques.* New York: Charles Scribner's Sons, 1966.

Miller, Judith and Martin, gen. ed. *Miller's Antiques Checklist: Porcelain.* Viking Studio Books. NY: Penguin Books USA Inc., 1991.

Moore, N. Hudson. *The Old China Book.* Rutland, Vt.: Charles E. Tuttle Company, 1986.

Nelson, Marion John. *Art Pottery of the Midwest.* Minneapolis: University Art Museum, University of Minnesota, 1988.

Ohrbach, Barbara Mila. *Antiques At Home: Cherchez's Book of Collecting and Decorating with Antiques.* New York: Clarkson N. Potter, Inc. 1989.

Pear, Lillian Myers. *The Pewabic Pottery: A History of Its Products and Its People.* Des Moines, Iowa: Wallace-Homestead Book Co., 1976.

Perry, Barbara, ed. *American Ceramics: The Collection of Everson Museum of Art.* New York: Rizzoli and Everson Museum of Art, 1989.

Plowden, Anna and Frances Halahan. *Looking After Antiques.* New York: Harper & Row, Publishers, 1988.

Preaud, Tamara and Serge Gauthier. *Ceramics of the Twentieth Century.* Oxford: Phaidon-Christie's Limited, 1982.

Ramsey, L. G. G., ed. *The Complete Color Encyclopedia of Antiques.* Preface by Bevis Hillier. Rev. ed. New York: Hawthorn Books, Inc., 1975.

Reed, Alan B. *Collector's Encyclopedia of Pickard China.* Paducah, Ky.: Collector Books, 1995.

Schlereth, Thomas J. *Victorian America: Transformations in Everyday Life, 1876 – 1915.* HarperPerennial Books. New York: HarperCollins Publishers, Inc., 1992.

Schwartz, Marvin D. and Richard Wolfe. *A History of American Art Porcelain.* New York: Renaissance Editions, 1967.

The National Committee to Save America's Cultural Collections. *Caring For Your Collections.* Foreword by Arthur W. Shultz, chairman. New York: Harry N. Abrams, Inc., Publishers, 1992.

Treadwell, John H. *A Manual of Pottery and Porcelain for American Collectors.* New York: G. P. Putnam & Sons, 1872.

Trimble, Alberta C. *Modern Porcelain: Today's Treasures, Tomorrow's Traditions.* New York: Harper & Brothers, 1962.

Wallace, Carol McD. *Victorian Treasures: An Album and Historical Guide for Collectors.* New York: Harry N. Abrams, Inc., 1993.

Watson, Lucilla. *Understanding Antiques.* Gallery Books. New York: W. H. Smith Publishers Inc., 1991.

Weiss, Peg, ed. *Adelaide Alsop Robineau: Glory in Porcelain.* Syracuse, N.Y.: Syracuse University Press, 1981.

Westropp, Hodder M. *Handbook of Pottery & Porcelain.* London: Chatto & Windus, 1880.

Wheatley, Henry B., F.S.A., and Philip H. Delamotte. *Art Work in Porcelain.* New York: Charles Scribner's Sons, 1883.

Wood, Serry. *Hand-Painted China.* How-to-do section by S. S. Frackelton. Watkins Glen, NY: Century House, 1953.

Winkler, Gail Caskey and Roger W. Moss. *Victorian Interior Decoration: American Interiors 1830 – 1900.* New York: Henry Holt and Company, 1986.

Yates, Raymond F. and Marguerite W. *A Guide to Victorian Antiques.* New York: Gramercy Publishing Company, 1949.

Zingman-Leith, Elan and Susan. *Creating Authentic Victorian Rooms.* Washington, DC: Elliott & Clark Publishing, 1995.

_____. *The Secret Life of Victorian Houses.* Washington, DC: Elliott & Clark Publishing, 1993.

# Articles

"Arts and Crafts Wed," *The Art Digest.* (November 15, 1943), 12.

Austin, John C. and Joseph Peter Spang. "Ceramics," *Antiques.* (March 1985), 670-675.

Berlew, Joyce. "Come Along and Paint with Me!: A Brief History of Porcelain Art," *The China Decorator.* (April 1989), 19-23.

Brandimarte, Cynthia A. "Somebody's Aunt and Nobody's Mother: The American China Painter and Her Work, 1870 – 1920," *Winterthur Portfolio.* Vol. 23, No. 4 (Winter 1988), 203-224.

Caldwell, Margaret. "In the American Mold: Pioneering Porcelains Reflect the Exuberance of an Emerging Nation," *HG.* (May 1989), 174-176, 214.

Clarke, Juliet and Florence. "Beautiful China Old and New for Modern Tables," *Arts & Decoration* (January 1932), 34-36, 73.

"Forum of Decorative Arts," *The Art News.* Vol. 33, No. 30 (April 27, 1935), 10.

Gibbons, John. "American Vogues in Porcelain Since Colonial Days," *Arts & Decoration* (February 1943), 6-7, 19.

Gardner, Dr. Bellamy. "Budding Porcelain Collector," *Apollo.* (April 1941), 98-100, and (November 1941), 133.

Good, Fay. "Thunder from Down Under: A Brief History of Ceramics. . .," *The China Decorator.* (October 1984), 9.

Grayson, June. "Delicate Matters: The Fine Art of China Painting," *Victorian Sampler.* (Spring 1990), 36-39.

Harris, Leon. "Pleasure Before Business: First Mildred Mottahedeh Collects Rare Porcelain; Then She Sells Fine Reproductions to the World," *Connoisseur.* (April 1986), 72-77.

Jackson, Mrs. Nevill. "Profiles on Porcelain," *Antiques.* (December 1934), 217- 219.

McKinley, Cameron Curtis. "The Artistry of Fine Porcelain," *Architectural Digest.* (December 1981), 172-180.

Mitchell, James R. "The American Porcelain Tradition," *Connoisseur.* (February 1972), 123-131.

Morris, Joan. "An ABC for Chinaware," *Art in America.* Vol. 48, No. 1 (Spring 1960), 80-120.

"Porcelain," *The Art Digest.* (December 15, 1934), 22.

Shelley, Donald A. "Henry Ford and the Museum: the Pottery and Porcelain," *Antiques.* (February 1958), 164-168.

Smith, Shirley. "Did You Know. . . Porcelain Firsts," *The China Decorator.* (November 1992), 29, and (January 1993), 28.

Smith-Walleck, Joan. "Traveling East to the Birthplace of Western Porcelain," *The Porcelain Artist.* (July/August 1992), 31, 46.

Timm, Ruth. "The Fine Art of Porcelain Painting," *The China Decorator.* (October 1984), 17-18.

Unn-Paye, Kari. "A Closer Look: Antique Porcelain," *The Porcelain Artist.* (November/December 1992), 40-41.

Williams, Ericka. "Did You Know There is No Such Thing as 'Dresden China'," *The Porcelain Artist.* (March/April 1992), 46-47.

## Technical

Charles, Bernard H. and David Charles. *Pottery and Porcelain: A Dictionary of Terms.* Newton, Great Britain: 1974. [publisher unknown]

Drury, Elizabeth, ed. *Antiques: Traditional Techniques of the Master Craftsmen.* Bloomsbury Books. London: MacMillan London Limited, 1986.

Herberts, Kurt. *The Complete Book of Artists' Techniques.* New York: Frederick A. Praeger, 1958.

Hughes, G. Bernard. *The Country Life Collector's Pocket Book of China.* Rev. ed. London: Country Life, 1977.

McLaughlin, M. Louise. *The China Painters' Hand Book.* The Practical Series I. Cincinnati: By the Author, 1917.

Meister, Peter Wilhelm and Horst Reber. *European Porcelain of the 18th Century.* Trans. Ewald Osers. Ithaca, N.Y.: Cornell University Press, 1980.

Monachesi, Mrs. Nicola di Rienzi. *A Manual for China Painters.* Boston: Lothrop, Lee & Shepard Co., 1907.

Rice, Prudence M. *Pottery Analysis.* Chicago: The University of Chicago Press, 1987.

Serfass, Ronald. *Porcelain: The Elite of Ceramics.* New York: Crown Publishers, Inc., 1979.

Southwell, Sheila. *Painting China and Porcelain.* Poole, Dorset, England: Blandford Press, 1980.

Vance-Phillips, L. *The Book of The China Painter.* New York: Montague Marks, 1896. Reprinted 1969 by G. Burbank.

# Alphabetical Listing of Artists and Studios

*Dates of signed pieces and known studio dates are included in parentheses.

# Index

*In conclusion, look upon this art not altogether as "a craze," or as a pastime — it is something nobler.*

Susan Stuart Goodrich Frackelton
Tried by Fire
(1885)

# COLLECTOR BOOKS

### Informing Today's Collector

*For over two decades we have been keeping collectors informed on trends and values in all fields of antiques and collectibles.*

## BOOKS ON GLASS AND POTTERY

| | | |
|---|---|---|
| 1810 | American Art Glass, Shuman | $29.95 |
| 1312 | Blue & White Stoneware, McNerney | $9.95 |
| 1959 | Blue Willow, 2nd Ed., Gaston | $14.95 |
| 4553 | Coll. Glassware from the 40's, 50's, 60's, 3rd Ed., Florence | $19.95 |
| 3816 | Collectible Vernon Kilns, Nelson | $24.95 |
| 3311 | Collecting Yellow Ware – Id. & Value Gd., McAllister | $16.95 |
| 1373 | Collector's Ency. of American Dinnerware, Cunningham | $24.95 |
| 3815 | Coll. Ency. of Blue Ridge Dinnerware, Newbound | $19.95 |
| 2272 | Collector's Ency. of California Pottery, Chipman | $24.95 |
| 3811 | Collector's Ency. of Colorado Pottery, Carlton | $24.95 |
| 3312 | Collector's Ency. of Children's Dishes, Whitmyer | $19.95 |
| 2133 | Collector's Ency. of Cookie Jars, Roerig | $24.95 |
| 3723 | Coll. Ency. of Cookie Jars-Volume II, Roerig | $24.95 |
| 4552 | Collector's Ency. of Depression Glass, 12th Ed., Florence | $19.95 |
| 2209 | Collector's Ency. of Fiesta, 7th Ed., Huxford | $19.95 |
| 1439 | Collector's Ency. of Flow Blue China, Gaston | $19.95 |
| 3812 | Coll. Ency. of Flow Blue China, 2nd Ed., Gaston | $24.95 |
| 3813 | Collector's Ency. of Hall China, 2nd Ed., Whitmyer | $24.95 |
| 2334 | Collector's Ency. of Majolica Pottery, Katz-Marks | $19.95 |
| 1358 | Collector's Ency. of McCoy Pottery, Huxford | $19.95 |
| 3313 | Collector's Ency. of Niloak, Gifford | $19.95 |
| 3837 | Collector's Ency. of Nippon Porcelain I, Van Patten | $24.95 |
| 2089 | Collector's Ency. of Nippon Porcelain II, Van Patten | $24.95 |
| 1665 | Collector's Ency. of Nippon Porcelain III, Van Patten | $24.95 |
| 4712 | Collector's Ency. of Nippon Porcelain IV, Van Patten | $24.95 |
| 1447 | Collector's Ency. of Noritake, 1st Series, Van Patten | $19.95 |
| 1034 | Collector's Ency. of Roseville Pottery, Huxford | $19.95 |
| 1035 | Collector's Ency. of Roseville Pottery, 2nd Ed., Huxford | $19.95 |
| 3314 | Collector's Ency. of Van Briggle Art Pottery, Sasicki | $24.95 |
| 2339 | Collector's Guide to Shawnee Pottery, Vanderbilt | $19.95 |
| 1425 | Cookie Jars, Westfall | $9.95 |
| 3440 | Cookie Jars, Book II, Westfall | $19.95 |
| 2275 | Czechoslovakian Glass & Collectibles, Barta | $16.95 |
| 4716 | Elegant Glassware of the Depression Era, 7th Ed., Florence | $19.95 |
| 3725 | Fostoria - Pressed, Blown & Hand Molded Shapes, Kerr | $24.95 |
| 3883 | Fostoria Stemware - The Crystal for America, Long | $24.95 |
| 3886 | Kitchen Glassware of the Depression Years, 5th Ed., Florence | $19.95 |
| 4772 | McCoy Pottery, Coll. Reference & Value Guide, Hanson | $19.95 |
| 4725 | Pocket Guide to Depression Glass, 10th Ed., Florence | $9.95 |
| 3825 | Puritan Pottery, Morris | $24.95 |
| 1670 | Red Wing Collectibles, DePasquale | $9.95 |
| 1440 | Red Wing Stoneware, DePasquale | $9.95 |
| 1958 | So. Potteries Blue Ridge Dinnerware, 3rd Ed., Newbound | $14.95 |
| 4634 | Standard Carnival Glass, 5th Ed., Edwards | $24.95 |
| 3327 | Watt Pottery – Identification & Value Guide, Morris | $19.95 |
| 2224 | World of Salt Shakers, 2nd Ed., Lechner | $24.95 |

## BOOKS ON DOLLS & TOYS

| | | |
|---|---|---|
| 4707 | A Decade of Barbie Dolls and Collectibles, 1981 - 1991, Summers | $19.95 |
| 2079 | Barbie Fashion, Vol. 1, 1959-1967, Eames | $24.95 |
| 3310 | Black Dolls – 1820 - 1991 – Id. & Value Guide, Perkins | $17.95 |
| 1529 | Collector's Ency. of Barbie Dolls, DeWein | $19.95 |
| 2338 | Collector's Ency. of Disneyana, Longest & Stern | $24.95 |
| 3727 | Coll. Guide to Ideal Dolls, Izen | $18.95 |
| 4645 | Madame Alexander Price Guide #21, Smith | $9.95 |
| 4723 | Matchbox Toys, 1947 to 1996, Johnson | $18.95 |
| 4647 | Modern Collector's Dolls, 8th series, Smith | $24.95 |
| 1540 | Modern Toys, 1930 - 1980, Baker | $19.95 |
| 4640 | Patricia Smith's Doll Values – Antique to Modern, 12th ed. | $12.95 |
| 4728 | Schroeder's Coll. Toys, 3rd Edition | $17.95 |
| 3826 | Story of Barbie, Westenhouser, No Values | $19.95 |
| 2028 | Toys, Antique & Collectible, Longest | $14.95 |
| 1808 | Wonder of Barbie, Manos | $9.95 |
| 1430 | World of Barbie Dolls, Manos | $9.95 |

## OTHER COLLECTIBLES

| | | |
|---|---|---|
| 1457 | American Oak Furniture, McNerney | $9.95 |
| 3716 | American Oak Furniture, Book II, McNerney | $12.95 |
| 4704 | Antique & Collectible Buttons, Wisniewski | $19.95 |
| 2333 | Antique & Collectible Marbles, 3rd Ed., Grist | $9.95 |
| 1748 | Antique Purses, Holiner | $19.95 |
| 1426 | Arrowheads & Projectile Points, Hothem | $7.95 |
| 1278 | Art Nouveau & Art Deco Jewelry, Baker | $9.95 |
| 1714 | Black Collectibles, Gibbs | $19.95 |
| 4708 | B.J. Summers' Guide to Coca-Cola, Summers | $19.95 |
| 1128 | Bottle Pricing Guide, 3rd Ed., Cleveland | $7.95 |
| 3717 | Christmas Collectibles, 2nd Ed., Whitmyer | $24.95 |
| 1752 | Christmas Ornaments, Johnson | $19.95 |
| 3718 | Collectible Aluminum, Grist | $16.95 |
| 2132 | Collector's Ency. of American Furniture, Vol. I, Swedberg | $24.95 |
| 2271 | Collector's Ency. of American Furniture, Vol. II, Swedberg | $24.95 |
| 3720 | Coll. Ency. of American Furniture, Vol III, Swedberg | $24.95 |
| 3722 | Coll. Ency. of Compacts, Carryalls & Face Powder Boxes, Mueller | $24.95 |
| 2018 | Collector's Ency. of Granite Ware, Greguire | $24.95 |
| 3430 | Coll. Ency. of Granite Ware, Book 2, Greguire | $24.95 |
| 1441 | Collector's Guide to Post Cards, Wood | $9.95 |
| 2276 | Decoys, Kangas | $24.95 |
| 1716 | Fifty Years of Fashion Jewelry, Baker | $19.95 |
| 4568 | Flea Market Trader, 10th Ed., Huxford | $12.95 |
| 3819 | General Store Collectibles, Wilson | $24.95 |
| 3436 | Grist's Big Book of Marbles, Everett Grist | $19.95 |
| 2278 | Grist's Machine Made & Contemporary Marbles | $9.95 |
| 1424 | Hatpins & Hatpin Holders, Baker | $9.95 |
| 4721 | Huxford's Collectible Advertising – Id. & Value Gd., 3rd Ed | $24.95 |
| 4648 | Huxford's Old Book Value Guide, 8th Ed. | $19.95 |
| 1181 | 100 Years of Collectible Jewelry, Baker | $9.95 |
| 2216 | Kitchen Antiques – 1790 - 1940, McNerney | $14.95 |
| 4724 | Modern Guns – Id. & Val. Gd., 11th Ed., Quertermous | $12.95 |
| 2026 | Railroad Collectibles, 4th Ed., Baker | $14.95 |
| 1632 | Salt & Pepper Shakers, Guarnaccia | $9.95 |
| 1888 | Salt & Pepper Shakers II, Guarnaccia | $14.95 |
| 2220 | Salt & Pepper Shakers III, Guarnaccia | $14.95 |
| 3443 | Salt & Pepper Shakers IV, Guarnaccia | $18.95 |
| 4727 | Schroeder's Antiques Price Guide, 15th Ed. | $14.95 |
| 4729 | Sewing Tools & Trinkets, Thompson | $24.95 |
| 2096 | Silverplated Flatware, 4th Ed., Hagan | $14.95 |
| 2348 | 20th Century Fashionable Plastic Jewelry, Baker | $19.95 |
| 3828 | Value Guide to Advertising Memorabilia, Summers | $18.95 |
| 3830 | Vintage Vanity Bags & Purses, Gerson | $24.95 |

# Schroeder's ANTIQUES Price Guide

. . . is the #1 best-selling antiques & collectibles value guide on the market today, and here's why . . .

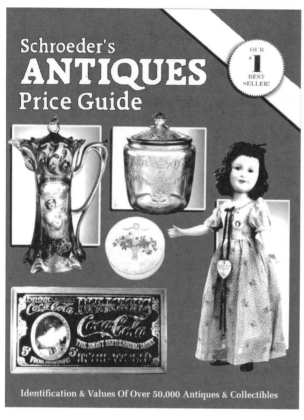

**Schroeder's ANTIQUES Price Guide**

OUR #1 BEST SELLER!

Identification & Values Of Over 50,000 Antiques & Collectibles

*8½ x 11, 608 Pages, $12.95*

• More than 300 advisors, well-known dealers, and top-notch collectors work together with our editors to bring you accurate information regarding pricing and identification.

• More than 45,000 items in almost 500 categories are listed along with hundreds of sharp original photos that illustrate not only the rare and unusual, but the common, popular collectibles as well.

• Each large close-up shot shows important details clearly. Every subject is represented with histories and background information, a feature not found in any of our competitors' publications.

• Our editors keep abreast of newly developing trends, often adding several new categories a year as the need arises.

If it merits the interest of today's collector, you'll find it in *Schroeder's*. And you can feel confident that the information we publish is up to date and accurate. Our advisors thoroughly check each category to spot inconsistencies, listings that may not be entirely reflective of market dealings, and lines too vague to be of merit. Only the best of the lot remains for publication.

Without doubt, you'll find
**SCHROEDER'S ANTIQUES PRICE GUIDE**
the only one to buy for
reliable information and values.

**COLLECTOR BOOKS**
*A Division of Schroeder Publishing Co., Inc.*